Intentional

life

Intentional

HOW

TO FINISH

WHAT YOU

START

Chris Bailey

PENGUIN LIFE

VIKING

An imprint of Penguin Random House LLC

1745 Broadway, New York, NY 10019

penguinrandomhouse.com

Copyright © 2026 by Chris Bailey

A Penguin Life Book

VIKING is a registered trademark of Penguin Random House LLC.
Line art by Anna Nativ.

Designed by Nerylsa Dijol

LIBRARY OF CONGRESS CONTROL NUMBER: 2025021924
ISBN 9780593833056 (hardcover)
ISBN 9780593833063 (ebook)

Printed in the United States of America
1st Printing

The authorized representative in the EU for product safety and compliance is Penguin Random House Ireland, Morrison Chambers, 32 Nassau Street, Dublin D02 YH68, Ireland, https://eu-contact.penguin.ie.

To my teachers—the scientists, educators, monks,
and mentors—who nurtured in me a sense of self-direction.
This book is for you.

CONTENTS

A Quick AI Statement

The other day, I was chatting with a friendly new acquaintance when he said something that took me aback: that he doesn't read books anymore. He used to love them but feels as though he now can't trust them in this age of artificial intelligence. After all, how can he be sure that a book was written by a human and not by some algorithm?

As an author of three books (and now four—welcome!), what he said surprised me. But on some level, I also agreed with him. As a reader, I want to know that an author didn't "phone it in"—that they wrote a book themselves. Hence, this short statement before we jump into the book.

The fundamental premise of this book is that the key to goal attainment is doubling down on how intentional we are. In this way, human intentionality is not only beautiful but also profoundly powerful. By turning our intentions into actions, we can go our own way to accomplish the things we truly want to get out of life. There is nothing wrong with automatic behavior—habits are extraordinarily powerful too, for example. But to attain many of our goals, we must act deliberately, with intention. That is what this book is about. While we perform around half of our actions out of habit (40 to 45 percent of them), this book is about the other half of our actions— the intentional half.[1]

As such, it felt plain wrong to use AI at all in writing this book.

I stubbornly didn't even run the manuscript through my grammar checker of choice, once I saw that it had introduced features powered by artificial intelligence. At the end of the day, I wanted to be able to say that I wrote this book, as I can with the others.

So, here's my quick AI statement: Every part of this book was written by me, Chris. (Except where it was edited by my lovely editors at Penguin Random House!)

The only exception is the notes section at the very back, which cites the research articles I read and referenced while writing this book. I love reading these papers, but I can't stand formatting the references for them. I didn't use AI to format these references because I got a hand with them from a colleague. (Thanks, Dana!) But if it weren't for her help, I honestly probably *would have* used AI. In the past, I couldn't stand this part of the writing process and would have been more than comfortable with its covering for me here.

This is, in my view, the rightful place that AI should have in our workflows. It should do the drudgery, not the art.

As this book goes to print, the dust is still settling with how these new technologies will affect books and, more broadly, the publishing industry. Not to mention other forms of art. My personal hope is that a book remains something that is handcrafted, not generated; that there is general repulsion for and rejection of art generated by AI that is passed off as being created by a human. Time will tell whether this will be the case, and a lot of dust still has to settle—but I have hope.

For now, though, I'll do my best to keep creating work that you will find practically useful and interesting. I'll be doing this work myself, standing not on the shoulders of machines but of researchers, scientists, and those who helped me along the way, who are thanked in the acknowledgments.

The humans.

0

Elusive Goals

When I was growing up, much to my chagrin, my parents always made me do one extracurricular sports-related activity. Honestly, they probably just wanted me to get out of the house. If I had things my way, I would have much preferred to stay home to read or program on the computer. But alas, I had to choose a sport. For a while, my sport of choice was karate—largely because the sensei who operated the local studio frequently canceled classes. After putting a bit more thought into it, though, I eventually took up golf.

I still remember the golf instructor I had. A middle-aged man with a notably gentle voice—which, for whatever reason, everyone in the game of golf seems to have—Bob taught me a lot about how to swing a club. Starting out, I could hardly hit the ball, even if I took a run at it Happy Gilmore–style. But by the end of my lessons with Bob, I'm glad to report that I could not only hit the ball every time I swung the club, I could hit it well! And far, and straight. (Thank you, Bob.)

The most interesting lesson Bob taught me was also the technique that improved my swing the most. Prior to taking lessons, when swinging the club, I considered my work done once I hit the ball. (Frankly, I was just relieved to have hit the damn thing.) But what Bob taught me was that the art of swinging a club is in focusing on what happens *after* I hit the ball, just as much as before. Prior to Bob, I had believed that the post-swing quarter pirouette, where you turn forward to look at your glorious shot, was a needless flourish that served only to make you look good. It turns out, the opposite is the case.

When you swing a club and it connects with the ball, your swing is not done—it's only half over. Focusing on what happened *after* my club made contact with the ball—and making sure my club moved in one uniform arc the whole way through—improved my swing dramatically. In focusing not on the windup but on the *follow-through*, I found myself actually hitting the ball more consistently.

The windup matters—but the follow-through matters just as much.

MY GOAL GRAVEYARD

A few years ago, I was impatient with my progress to achieve my goal of learning to play the piano. I found myself looking back at the graveyard of goals I had tried and failed to achieve. A curious pattern seemed to emerge. While I'd had no problem starting and even maintaining my progress, what I hadn't managed to do was follow through—especially on my long-term goals.

I can't count the number of times I have set a goal to lose a certain number of pounds, only to fall back into the same habits and routines, gaining it back again. Or the number of times I've carved out a wonderful daily running ritual, only to have it fade over time. On the floor of our basement are numerous home gym contraptions that I bought once and used religiously—for a month or two before stopping forever.

Setting goals? No problem. Making detailed plans for how to achieve my goals and being productive with them on a regular basis? Also not a problem. But caring about them over a long period of time? And consistently actioning them so I could make decent progress over the long term? As far as I can look back, that has proven *much* more difficult.

In the last decade of studying and writing about personal productivity, I've read too many books and research articles on productivity to count. Yet, despite all this research, over time, my graveyard of forgotten goals has only gotten more crowded.

And so, I started to ask *why*.

Why do some goals feel effortless, while others feel like a chore?

Why do certain goals feel continually and stubbornly beyond our reach, no matter how hard we try?

How does goal setting—and, more important, goal attainment—even work? How *should* it work?

What does the research say about how we can follow through with our goals more often?

How can we make our goals more meaningful—so much so that they feel completely natural, an extension of who we are?

What does it take for us to actually follow through with the goals and intentions we set?

THE KEY TO FOLLOWING THROUGH

As I started digging into these questions, I chatted with researchers, scientists, and even Buddhist monks, and found these answers and more. I'll share a rather large spoiler right now: **The key to finishing what you start is becoming more intentional.** For this reason, intentionality is a primary focus of this book—alongside goal attainment.

Becoming more intentional—deciding what to do before doing

it—sometimes gets a bad rap, and for a good reason. We don't always follow through with the intentions that we set. Much as some of us who have a graveyard of exercise equipment that we aspirationally keep in the basement, we have a similar wasteland of failed intentions that collect dust in our mind.

Here's a bit of weight off your shoulders, though: This is normal. To be expected, even. It's simply human to set intentions but not follow through to reach the goals we set. Fortunately for us all, however, there is concrete science behind how we can follow through on our intentions every day, week, or year, and throughout our lives. In the process, intention remains central to attaining our goals because **when we do follow through, an intention always came first**. For example, we don't always go for a morning run after we plan to—sometimes life gets in the way, other times, we can't muster up the motivation. But when we do go for a run, it's because we had originally set an intention to do so.

In other words, intention is the mental process that precedes our actually doing anything, including making progress on our goals. It's integral to goal attainment because it creates action.

There is a fascinating magic to the idea and practice of intentionality. We all have things we desire to accomplish—whether that's drinking more water throughout the day, running a marathon, or writing a book. Each of us has intentions of every shape and size and intensity: large and small, difficult and easy, and meaningful and shallow.

To borrow a sports reference that you've likely heard one too many times before, intention is a kind of Wayne Gretzky *you miss one hundred percent of the shots you don't take* situation. You won't always follow through with your intentions. But if you never set any intentions, you won't achieve any of what you want.

Generally, the more intentions you set, the better you'll do. The longer, extended Gretzky quote is "You miss one hundred percent of the shots you don't take, even though there's only a 1 to 5 percent [probability] of scoring."[1] Luckily for us, intentions provide us with a far higher probability of success—and it's possible to set stronger intentions that lead us to follow through with our goals far more often.

We'll cover how to do this over the course of this book.

THIS BOOK FROM TEN THOUSAND FEET

I write about the subject of personal productivity in my previous books—a topic that goal attainment is tangentially related to. For many, the topic of personal productivity conjures up cold, corporate imagery. But if you're familiar with my previous work, you know I approach things differently. To me, productivity is all about becoming more deliberate and intentional in how we work and live our lives.

If productivity is about intention, then by this definition **we're perfectly productive when we do what we set out to do**—whether that's being deeply present in a coffee shop conversation with a friend, settling into a beach lounge chair with a good book, or clawing our way back to "inbox zero" by the end of a busy week. In a way, productivity can be seen as the process of following through with the tiny, short-term goals we set on a daily basis.

As you know, following through with our intentions is far easier said than done. If our intentions and goals suddenly became easy, this book would not need to exist. Productivity books—or at least the helpful ones!—would also vanish into a *poof* of smoke. Yet as you have already found, there is something about our goals and sticking with our intentions that proves fundamentally elusive. At any one time, we all have a set of things we want to accomplish: whether that's meeting work deadlines, losing weight, or even finishing this book. There are many reasons we don't finish what we start. Some tasks and goals may prove too aversive (difficult and ugly) and others too time-consuming, while others get crowded out by the throes of everyday life. If you've gotten distracted from this book, you may also know that we often don't even notice intentions to do new and different things as they form—even when they completely derail our attention. It's no wonder, as the saying goes, that the "road to hell is paved with good intentions."

The good news is that it doesn't have to be this way. So let's get on a *different* road and actually follow through with the goals and intentions that we set.

We'll cover significant ground throughout this book, so let me show you the book from ten thousand feet, to give you a loose framework to keep in mind as you read. Some of the ideas we'll discuss include:

- **Where intentions come from.** We'll break down the differences between our "default" intentions and "deliberate" intentions. Anyone can follow through with the intentions they set by default—and as you'll see, it's also often a nice break to "go with the flow." But we unlock more of what intention has to offer us when we take charge of our actions to go our own way. In the process, our time becomes significantly more productive and meaningful.

- **Human values.** Simply put, our values are the motivational bedrock that also drives everything we do. By understanding our values, we can craft intentions that feel like a natural extension of who we are. According to the latest research, there are twelve basic, fundamental human values that we all share to some extent—and the science behind them has been validated across hundreds of thousands of study participants, cross-culturally in more than eighty countries. Using these twelve basic values as a starting point, we can construct intentions in a way that leads us to significantly greater goal attainment and meaning. I'll share some values rituals that I personally use that can help us all live more in accordance with what we value every day, including practicing what I call "intentional indulgence," knowing what your "opposing values" are, and measuring how you spend your time relative to your innermost values. Values may sound like a mushy topic, but as you'll quickly see, they're central to the science of goal attainment—assuming you follow the science.

- **Why and when we should drop (or "edit") the goals we have already set.** Over time, the more goals we abandon, the more other goals we get to try on for size. Some goals are worth sticking with, while others are worth dropping. Chapter 3 will help you distinguish between them.

- **What makes some goals and intentions downright aversive.** It turns out there are specific attributes that make some goals, and the actions we must take to achieve them, aversive. The six attributes of aversion also lead us to procrastination, a phenomenon we can overcome by understanding and compensating for the aversion that is embedded within our goals.

- **The "antecedents of desire" and how to cultivate them.** These are the attributes a goal or action can have that make us significantly more likely to follow through with it. Just as there are attributes of aversion, there are characteristics of a goal that make it more desirable. Every goal has some combination of both aversion and desire. By cultivating desire, the things we wish to accomplish become more attractive to do—which naturally makes us more likely to do them.

- **"Intention rituals."** These are the rituals we can invest in that lead us to follow through on our goals more often: carving out "islands of intentions" throughout our day, the technique of "mental contrasting," adding structured accountability habits into our day, and more.

Practicing forethought through rituals like these is akin to building a moat around your intentions—the process fortifies what you wish to accomplish so you'll actually follow through with it.

By the end of this book, my goal is to provide you with the ideas and techniques that you need to do the things that you set out to do. In the process, you'll learn to craft smarter goals and intentions that are personalized to *who you are*, which will make you follow through on them more often.

SCIENCE HELP

Before we jump in, just a few more quick notes for you to keep in mind.

First, a word of advice on . . . advice. As this book explores the subject of personal productivity (among other topics), it's worth mentioning that personal productivity is just that: personal. As such, not all the ideas in this book will resonate with you.

In my opinion, this is a good thing. But for this reason, **be sure to take the ideas in this book that work for you and leave the rest**. Try as many of the ideas here as you can. They have made it into the book because according to the latest science—and a little personal experience—they work. Be prepared to be surprised by what works and what doesn't. And experiment, experiment, experiment.

Wherever possible, this book is based on scientific evidence. There is a literal treasure trove of research that has been conducted on the subject of goal attainment—and as I discovered reading through it, it's as fascinating as it is inspiring. Productivity advice that isn't rooted in research has always confused me: What *is* it rooted in? Wishful thinking? Hopes and dreams? Unicorn dust? (That last one doesn't sound too bad, actually.) It just makes sense to me that any advice on how we should live our life should be grounded in evidence—or, at the bare minimum, personal experience of what works. A lot of advice that sounds good on the surface doesn't hold water in practice (I'll share a story or two about this later in the book).

I am not a scientist by training. That said, one of my weird passions is devouring journal articles about productivity and other interesting topics—to connect disparate ideas from research, experts, and, in this book, even Buddhist monks. While writing this book, I pored over thousands and read hundreds of studies related to topics like goal attainment, intentionality, aversion, desire, and values, all to filter through the prevailing evidence about what actually works. I simply find productivity techniques grounded in scientific research to be more worthy of our time—and more interesting. As you read this, I hope you do, too. I've done my best to do as much work as possible on your behalf.

The research that I reference in this book is cited in the notes chapter at the back of the book. If you find an idea in this book compelling, I encourage you to flip to this section to see where the idea comes from. (I've left the endnote references formatted as superscript in case you're curious to check any of them out.) This way, you can learn more about the research papers that I cite—if an idea interests you, the original research paper may also interest you. (Though reading research papers is obviously not for everyone!)

There are exercises sprinkled throughout these pages—isolated activities you can try that reinforce many of the concepts in this book. You don't have to do any of them if you don't want to, but I've designed each to allow you to extract more value from the ideas I will talk about. If doing them will interrupt your flow of reading, don't worry: The very last chapter of the book will provide you with a roadmap for putting all the tactics in the book into practice. Feel free to "choose your own adventure" in reading the book: I've done my best to structure it to be helpful to you, regardless of how you want to read it. Most of the exercises will help you earn back time, just like the tactics will.

Real work is more complicated than what can take place inside a laboratory. My hope is that by keeping one foot in the research, and one foot in the tactical implementations of it, this book will serve as an effective bridge between both for you.

Okay, that's enough preamble. Now that you have both the lay of the land with the chapters to come, as well as a general idea of my approach to writing this book, let's dig in.

We'll start by exploring a subject I find absolutely fascinating: where intention comes from.

A Note on Accomplishment

An unfortunate truth about productivity advice is that it often makes you feel as though you're not doing enough. In trying to become more productive, we tend to focus on our deficiencies—like how little we're getting done every day and how many goals we have yet to achieve. Focusing on achieving more, it's easy to feel like we're not achieving enough.

For this reason, in striving to become more productive, we should remind ourselves of all the fruits our efforts have led to in the past.

My favorite way to do this is to keep an "accomplishments list." The definition is in the name: It's a list of everything you've accomplished. You can keep the list across whatever timeline you'd like. If you find yourself dragging your heels to get things done throughout the week, capture the things, large and small, that you accomplish throughout that week to review alongside your intentions. If you instead prefer to reflect on the larger results of your labor, update a list of the results your efforts have led to—at work and at home—throughout the year. I prefer to keep the yearly list, and often also keep a weekly list when I'm feeling especially unmotivated. Like a well-structured goal, both lists are great motivational propellant.

Often in the journey to become more productive, our negative self-talk goes through the roof as we try to change how we work and live. In considering what you have yet to achieve, remember all that you have achieved already—this counterbalances negative self-talk, while letting you remind yourself of all the great things you've done so far.

Intentional

1

The Intention Stack

"We look at the world once,
in childhood. The rest is memory."
—*Louise Glück*[1]

Thimation—whether it is deliberate or automatic—is intentionality.

An intention is simply a mental plan to do something. It doesn't have to be deliberate or even conscious. As researchers have put it, "Environmental features can activate automatic [intentions] that affect goal-directed cognition and behavior without conscious awareness." These intentions "produce similar performance outcomes as conscious" goals.[2]

In other words: We set intentions with and without meaning to, based on conditions in our environment and in our mind.

THE SOURCES OF INTENTION

One day, while working on this book, I attended a talk by a Buddhist monk.* At the time, I was knee-deep in the research about where

---

*I won't identify the monk by his name, as the monastery where he resides responded that he does not participate in media interviews (including being interviewed for this book). I hope you'll forgive if my referring to him as "the monk" gets a bit impersonal. He's thanked in the acknowledgments, if you're curious.

intention arises from. I obviously didn't expect that the monk would have brushed up on this particular topic, and he probably hadn't. Monks tend to look within to find answers—to the causes and effects within the mind—rather than outward to research papers. But as both approaches study causes and effects, it's no surprise that they sometimes arrive at the same results. So, on a whim, I decided to ask him the question I had been pondering: Where do our intentions come from?

On the surface, Buddhism and productivity have nothing in common. But at their core, both are about our relationship with intentionality—becoming more deliberate about our actions lives at the heart of both. This is not a book about Buddhism, of course, though the practice does give us a peek into how we can observe the intentions we set—including through meditative practices, many of which investigate the inner workings of the mind.

His answer coincided perfectly with what the research on intentionality has found. Actually, in some ways, he provided a *better* summary than the research currently can. According to the monk—and researchers—intentions arise from the following:

- **our biology** (e.g., when we set an intention to make a pit stop at the very next restroom we find while on a road trip),

- **the social environments that we're a part of** (e.g., when we set an intention to join our friends for a drink after work on Friday night—especially after a stressful week),

- **our conditioning by family or culture** (e.g., when we scarf down meals around the dinner table as quickly as our parents used to when we were growing up),

- **our desire to find happiness and avoid pain** (e.g., when we set an intention to ask someone out on a first date when we feel the need for companionship in our life),

- **the lessons we have learned** in the past (e.g., when we set an intention to have a frank conversation with a colleague after we took a workshop about more skillful conversation techniques), and

- **our "self-reflective capacity."** This is our ability to look within ourselves to consider the best way to proceed (e.g., when we stop to reflect on exactly what we want to get out of a busy week).

As you can see, we decide to do things—whether consciously or subconsciously—for a whole host of reasons.

On top of the sources of intention within us, there are also *characteristics* we can have that affect what kinds of intentions (and goals) we set. For example, those of us who are highly conscientious tend to make more ambitious plans. The more positively you regard yourself, the more competitive you are, and the better your general mood, the more challenging your intentions tend to be as well.[3]

While becoming more intentional is the key to goal attainment, it is remarkable how elusive our intentions can be. Examining where our intentions come from is tricky—but fascinating and informative. We set intentions constantly—to do everything from tying our shoelaces to starting a business. But a great number of these intentions slip by our notice.

Slippery Intentions

Here's a quick challenge for you. It won't take any time, though it may consume a bit of your attention. The next time your mind forms an intention to put down this book and do something else, try to notice that it has done so.

(continued)

Often the new intention will take the form of an *urge* to do something else. Imagine sitting down in your favorite chair and luxuriating in the sounds of your favorite playlist. If you were to pause the playlist midway through and sit in silence for a moment or two, you would eventually feel a new intention form— the next song you want to listen to. Your mind is forming new intentions like these all the time—you're just not always aware that it is doing so.

If you do manage to catch your next intention forming, try asking a simple question: What led your new intention to form? Try to examine the chain of events that led to the new intention. This might prove to be nearly impossible in the moment. But try.

For example:

- Was a certain passage of the book boring, which made you restless and want to do something else? (If so, apologies!)

- Did the sudden urge to do something else erupt in your mind—whether because you wanted to distract and stimulate your mind, or to get something else done apart from reading this book?

- Did your mind wander to other things as you were reading—despite your original intention to read this book—and this led you to think of something else to do?

- Did someone come into the room and interrupt your reading or ask you for help with something?

- Did a telemarketer call, leading you to forget about the book and start mindlessly scrolling through apps on your phone?

Intentions are fascinating, yet slippery. We set them all day, often without even noticing. Every time we take action in the service of some goal, we are acting out an intention that we have set. Sometimes intentions form as a result of previous conditioning. Other times, we construct them more deliberately, through conscious deliberation and selection. They come in all shapes and sizes.

Pay attention to the next intention you form—the next intention that derails your *current* intention, to follow through with reading this book.

Because so many of our intentions are formed automatically—beneath what we can notice with conscious awareness—this exercise can be far trickier than you might think.

THE TWO TYPES OF INTENTIONS

By default, we're happiness-seeking beings who want to find greater pleasure and avoid discomfort and pain. As we make decisions over time that get us to a place of greater comfort and happiness, our mind becomes conditioned—by ourselves and others—to respond in a certain way to events around us. Feeling lonely, we ask our future spouse out on a first date; seeing a delicious meal in front of us, we scarf it down quickly; feeling the urge to go to the bathroom on a road trip, we eagerly try to find the next possible stop.

Researchers have found that this conditioning typically springs forward out of our "neural autopilot mode"—the mental mode we deploy whenever we simply respond automatically to what comes our way. This mode runs our behavior when we don't take active control over our intentions.[4] Without conditions, nothing can arise at all.

The intentions we set because of this conditioning are our **default intentions**. Think about it. If you woke up one morning and didn't think through any of your actions, you'd still find yourself doing, well . . . things! They might not be the *ideal* things, and you may not find greater meaning, accomplishment, or happiness because of them. But you'd still spend your time in some way or another. (You would have to—even if you just lay in bed all day! An intention to do nothing all day is still an intention, albeit one that takes place over an entire day.)

In fact, research describes an interesting split between how much of our daily behavior is automatic and deliberate. Our default intentions drive much of what we do throughout the day: A whopping 40 to 45 percent of our daily actions are automatic. (Intentional activity rooted in volition makes up the other 55 to 60 percent of our behavior.) Default intentions not only prove immensely powerful—they also illustrate the broader place that intention has in our days and in our life.

Another way to understand default intentions: They make up our habits. Habits outsource the act of setting intentions to automatic processes within our brain. This means we don't have to think about them while our brain follows through with them on its neural autopilot mode. This is precisely what makes them so powerful.

If you have a habit of drinking a delicious, piping hot cup of coffee every morning right after you wake up, and you encounter the familiar conditions that trigger this habit (that is, you just got out of bed, your energy is low, and the day of the week ends with the letter *y*), your brain will form a plan to make a cup of coffee—all on your behalf! It's not as good as having a barista at home, but it gets you close. You don't even have to be awake enough to notice.

With enough awareness (and maybe also coffee), we can even observe our brain setting an intention to do the things we do without much thought. Twenty minutes into lying in bed bouncing between apps, we can observe that there is an urge that comes from within us to spring out of bed, get off our phone, and make our morning cup. (Buddhist monks often refer to this specific brand of motivation as "habit energy.")

Every habit is triggered by some default intention that we have formed in response to one of the five "habit cues" that have been identified by researchers: a certain time, place, preceding event, emotional state, or presence of certain people.[5] These environmental cues are what draw out our default intentions: Just as our default intentions lead us to act on autopilot, the conditions we encounter across these five categories trigger our intentions in the first place.

There is nothing wrong with our default intentions, and, in fact, relying on them can serve us quite well. Habits are remarkably powerful when we deploy them strategically, like when we develop focus routines to work more deeply throughout the day. It's also nice not to have to think too much about other habits, like the fact that we need to brush our teeth as part of our nightly wind-down ritual.

But when it comes to the attainment of most goals, **our default intentions are not enough**. We still need some level of deliberateness to chart our own way in work and life. It is through becoming more deliberate with the intentions we set that we take greater control of our actions—which provides us with room to do things *differently*—and in the process, grow and break out of the mold of our conditioning. Doing this, we can separate ourselves from habits that are no longer serving us and act in a way that makes us more productive. We can spend our time in a way that gives our days more meaning.

To create meaningful change, we can't simply rely on the same default intentions we always have relied on in the past. We must also set deliberate intentions.

SETTING DELIBERATE INTENTIONS

For a second, visualize some captivating movie montage of a protagonist going through the same dull, humdrum motions of their everyday life until they reach some critical tipping point and overhaul their entire life in some dramatic fit of awakening. They decide to quit their dead-end job and spend every hour of the day making music. Or they turn off the TV to sell their belongings and live in the Himalayas. Or they revamp their entire fitness regimen (which, of course, may even lead to a second, even more badass montage).

These are dramatic examples, but you get the point. Though our daily fits of awakening are typically far less dramatic, by a certain point, we all desire to search within ourselves to determine what we should do next—and differently. In that moment, we snap out of our default intentions to craft intentions that jibe more with who we are and who we wish to become. We remember something we've learned and set an intention to change the way we've always done things. Or we search within ourselves to find the motivation that will let us rise to the level of what is called for in the moment. Or we set goals for other choices we wish to make in our life.

This is where deliberate intentions come in. Unlike default intentions, deliberate intentions are ones we construct ourselves, rather than ones that arise because of our environment and previous conditioning.[6]

While good habits provide the foundation for a good life, intentionality allows us to remain in control and course correct along the way, so we can extract greater productivity and meaning out of our days—while following through more often. (Going forward, when I refer to intention, I'll be referring to our *deliberate* intentions.)

As I mentioned, intention lives at the heart of productivity. It is through setting deliberate intentions that we can reorient ourselves toward what's truly important as we work, rather than just being hyperefficient at responding to email or attending to whatever task is in front of us.

There is a great return to be found in becoming more intentional in our work. At work, not all our activities are created equal: We accomplish an inordinate amount through some of them, while we get very little done through others. For example, compare training an intern you've hired to help you with your workload with sitting through a meeting that's a complete and utter waste of everyone's time. For every minute you spend training and mentoring your new employee, you'll make several back, because they'll be able to do your work for you. Conversely, you'll make zero minutes back with the pointless meeting.

When much of our work is cognitively complex, it requires a thoughtful approach as much as it does speed. For example, how can you write that research paper in a way that it gets published in a reputable journal? Or how can you structure that briefing in a way that saves everyone time? Becoming more intentional in your approach to tasks like these makes you remarkably more productive. (At the same time, the habits you have formed provide you with the foundation of routines and rituals to help get the work done.)

This tendency and ability to look within to reflect on what we should do is our "self-reflective capacity" at work—a powerful and, frankly, quite beautiful capability of our mind. Our self-reflective capacity is our ability to look within ourselves so we can set different intentions from the ones we naturally feel inclined to set by default—while taking responsibility for and ownership of our actions.* [7]

In setting intentions that diverge from our defaults, we are able to choose what we would like to do next. We then set goals for what we would like to change or do differently.

HOW PRODUCTIVITY, GOALS, AND PROJECTS FIT INTO THE PICTURE

Before we go on, let's define a few terms we'll use throughout the book. Because not all tasks are created equal, becoming more intentional is key to accomplishing our goals. Every time we choose to do one thing over another, we can make a decision, as the saying goes, to "work smarter instead of harder." This lets us make back time and become more productive. This is why I view **productivity** as simply accomplishing what we intend to do.

Goals, on the other hand, are what our intentions have the potential to lead us to. I see a goal simply as something we are striving to accomplish. Setting a goal leads us to form smaller intentions. For example, a goal to lose five pounds of body fat may lead to intentions to drive to the gym, or an even smaller intention once we get there—to go for a run on the treadmill after we're done lifting weights.

Projects are worth discussing briefly as well. A project is a goal that has an end point, usually some deliverable that we need to make

---

*Curiously, it is not only humans that have this capability—dolphins and many apes also possess an ability to pass tests for self-awareness. For example, they can recognize themselves in mirrors. Researchers have also found that dolphins are able to practice metacognition—they're able to think about their thinking. They're also the only mammal, apart from humans, "shown capable of extensive and rich vocal and behavioral mimicry."

a reality—like a software application we're developing, an event we're planning, or a room in our house that we're renovating. Projects typically lead to specific outcomes and are more likely to involve other people—and we usually need to set quite a few intentions in order to achieve them. While we may have an intention to complete a project, projects themselves are not intentions—they're instead a series of actions we'll need to take in order to create something over a certain timeline.

THE SHAPE OF INTENTION

Let's lay a bit more land.

Each intention has a few attributes that define its structure. The first, as we've learned, is its **source**: our biology, social environment, cultural and social conditioning, our desire to find happiness and avoid pain, lessons we've learned, and our self-reflective capacity.

The second is its **duration**. The things we intend to get done can span basically any possible length of time: everything from taking another sip of coffee (five seconds), to being the kind of person who gives back to those around you (the rest of your life), to leaving a legacy that lasts until the heat death of the universe (good luck). The intentions we set vary considerably in how long they will take to follow through.

The third, and perhaps most important element for our purposes, is its **strength**. This is something we'll dive headfirst into in this book, because the stronger our intentions, the more likely we are to follow through with them.

The strength of an intention is a function of our desire minus our aversion. Every single task has some amount of both. Desire compels us to do something, while aversion drives us away from doing that thing—and in the process leads us to procrastinate.

Compare doing your taxes with watching a marathon of your favorite show. Both might have the same duration, and you may do both as a result of setting a deliberate intention. But while you probably prefer watching the TV marathon, the thought of doing your taxes might make you feel like, to use another overly dramatic cosmic analogy, throwing the Earth into the sun. (I'll be here all evening.) We inevitably must muster enough desire to do our taxes, because we desire to avoid the negative penalties of not doing them. Similarly, we often also have a bit of aversion to spending our time in a way that's overindulgent—which often manifests as guilt. (Fortunately for us, we can minimize the guilt that arises from this kind of indulgence by practicing intentional indulgence—an idea I cover in chapter 6.)

There is a lot we will unpack over the course of the book about both aversion and desire—particularly with how to minimize aversion and maximize desire. Believe it or not, with enough forethought, doing your taxes can be as compelling an activity as watching a marathon of your favorite show. Right now, though, just know that every intention you set, no matter the duration, contains some combination of desire and aversion—and that these ingredients directly affect how much you will want to follow through with the thing, whatever it is. If you find some of your goals far less attractive to tackle than others, know there are ways to remedy this.

A fourth attribute of an intention is its **depth**, which is how connected an intention is with what we value. The more connected a goal is with what we value dearly and deeply, the more motivated we'll be to get it done. For example, if you deeply value staying healthy, implementing a new exercise regimen will prove easier than if you don't. Conversely, if you value cooperation and need to prepare for an upcoming debate, you're more likely to put it off than someone who values power and dominance.

Values are best thought of as our deepest and broadest intentions, the guiding principles of our life that are also the most powerful motivational force that can propel our actions forward. Values also live at the core of who we are. When we can notice ourselves manifesting our values through our actions, we feel as though what we're doing is meaningful. (We'll explore the twelve fundamental human values in more detail in chapter 2.)

It is the structure of our intentions—default to deliberate—small and grand, that guides everything we do throughout the day and throughout our life.

THE INTENTION STACK

In addition to deliberateness, duration, strength, and depth, there is one other way our intentions are structured. Intentions don't just have characteristics of their own: They also exist relative to one other. Specifically, **intentions are nested inside one another.** Therein lies the key to following through on our most important goals.

For example, you may have an intention that spans decades to accomplish impactful things in your career while also helping others. Nested inside this might be a shorter intention to expand your business into a new market over the next twelve months and to launch a new product. Inside of *these* may be smaller intentions still, like to chat with your investors this afternoon or to find a retail partner for the launch. Inside of *these* may be the teensiest intentions of all, to dial in to a conference call or to ask your assistant to book a flight for you to meet with a potential new retailer.

We can visualize how our current actions fit together as a "stack" of sorts—where all our current goals are nested inside of one another. In the illustration below, our present-moment intentions are at the bottom. Our intentions that take place over an increasingly longer timeline are our "plans," "goals," "priorities," and "values." All have a place in the Intention Stack.

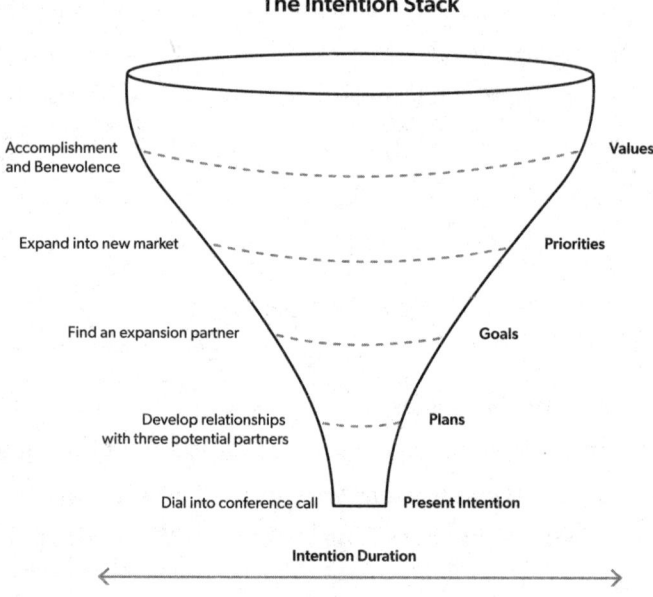

The Intention Stack

Let's return to the previous example of growing your business. Let's say that, at this moment, you're about to dial in to a conference call to chat with a potential business partner that you'll be flying to meet in person next week. At this one point in time, there can be several different intentions guiding your behavior, all nested within one another. There's your present intention to dial in to the call. There's the intention that this fits *inside of* to develop a relationship with the potential partner. Maybe *this* intention fits inside one to attain a goal you have defined, like to develop three partnerships through which you can grow your business. Then there's your even broader intention—which we can call a priority—to expand your business into new markets.

All these intentions may nest inside your values of accomplishment and benevolence (more on these and our other values in a second)—so you can achieve more while giving back to others.

Every moment of our day, there is a similar stack that exists on top of our actions, whether we're tying our shoelaces before running some errands or focusing in on developing a business plan. Therefore, the farther up and down the Intention Stack we consider our goals, the more likely we are to achieve them. We make sure our goal is constructed in a way that properly fits into our life, connecting who we are (values) with our daily actions.

Later in the book, we'll cover how to construct an Intention Stack like the one in the most recent illustration. We'll do so by considering how to stack the various levels of intentionality, which makes our goals significantly more motivating. In considering how our intentions are nested within one another, we color the full picture of each of our goals.

Working our way down through the Intention Stack, it is possible to consider all the intentions that might be nested within one another:

- Which of our **strongest values** our goal is most connected with.

- Which of our broader life's **priorities** the goal fits inside of.

- What our **goal** even is—in particular, what outcome we are trying to produce.

- Which series of **plans** will produce the defined outcome.

- What **next steps** we will need to take in order to make progress.

Over the course of this book, we'll work our way up this Intention Stack. We'll talk about both our goals and the intentions that they lead to. Then, we'll work our way through how to make them more of a priority in our life—by minimizing aversion and maximizing desire. Finally, we'll cover some rituals for taking action on our goals and values on a regular basis. But first, we'll talk about our values, which live at the top of the stack.

VALUES: THE HEART OF
THE INTENTION STACK

In a perfect world, our momentary intentions are always connected with what we most deeply value. But, of course, as we all know, not all our actions are deeply meaningful. While it is true that not every one of our actions will be rooted in our deepest values, the truth is that our actions are always rooted in *some* value. This includes when that value is not something we have in spades.

There are twelve fundamental values that represent a complete motivational continuum of what drives our behavior. They are: conformity, security, tradition, self-direction, stimulation, power, achievement, benevolence, universalism, pleasure, humility, and face. (Don't worry: We'll cover these ideas in detail in the next chapter. There's comprehensive and fascinating research behind what we value, as you'll quickly learn.)

Values are a crucial part of the Intention Stack. There is always some value—in most cases, multiple values—that are guiding our actions. Interestingly, the research shows that the intentions we feel most compelled to set in the moment are often the result of which of our values win out over others. One night, our values of pleasure and stimulation may win out as we indulge in a drink or two at a celebratory dinner. A different night, our values of self-direction and security might win out, as we use our autonomy to make an independent decision to prioritize our health instead.

The most meaningful course of action—to us in the moment, anyway—is always the one most aligned with our values. To continue with the night out example, maybe you value conformity and tradition far more than self-direction, and so the thought of turning down a good time with your friends for "some notion of independence" is baffling to you. Or maybe the opposite is true, and you value your independence and health so much that the thought of "poisoning your body" just to loosen up in a social situation is equally baffling. The strongest disagreements between us—and within ourselves—occur when our polar opposite values collide. (Which is why, as a culture, oh so many of the debates we have take place on top of opposing values, like those of tradition and progress.)

When we have autonomy over our time, we calculate the trade-offs between our own varying (and sometimes opposing) values and make the decision that maximizes pleasure and minimizes pain. Our innermost, most closely held default intentions—our strongest values—have space to win out when we have autonomy over our time.

This is partly why our behavior often feels less meaningful when we have less control. Instead of having the space to act in accordance with our values and who we are, our actions are chosen for us by the situation at hand. We don't always have as much autonomy as we would like: Sometimes our boss drops a big assignment on our desk early on a Friday afternoon or the snow outside needs to get shoveled when you'd much rather stay inside. In situations like these, our time can feel less meaningful, because we can no longer observe ourselves acting in the way we find most meaningful. Meaningful memories work similarly: We filter events through our deepest values and extract meaning accordingly.

Because our personal values form a complete motivational spectrum of anything and everything that could possibly be propelling our behavior forward at a given time, they are always there, underlying what we do. Therefore, aligning our goals with what we truly desire—aka our values—is how we follow through on them more often. Building an Intention Stack is what helps us do this.

NOTICING YOUR DEFAULTS

As we'll discuss in the next chapter, our values and default intentions are fundamentally linked. While we'll spend most of this book on our deliberate intentions, it's worth connecting with our defaults before diving deep into what we value. As we do, it can be tempting to write off how we act by default when we're doing things in autopilot mode. But the reality is more nuanced. There is immense power, and even freedom, in being on autopilot. Not to mention, when we act in a way that is by rote and automatic, we give our mind a chance to properly rest and recharge. (Not every moment of our every day has to be about productivity—and for the sake of our mental health, it probably *shouldn't* be.)

This autopilot mode is especially informative when we take a bit of time to notice our intentions forming. On the surface, this may seem like an odd or pointless exercise. Yet, our default intentions make up how we act throughout the day, all the actions we take when we don't choose to act deliberately. Any action you take on autopilot is guided by your default intentions. Noticing these intentions form, you can better understand just how many intentions make up how you already act—a big part of who you already are.

The key is to **take notice of your actions as you perform them**.

Doing this all the time would quickly get tiring. But it's possible to do this in small, deliberate bursts. The best way I have found for noticing (and taking greater advantage of) our default intentions is by practicing mindfulness. Mindfulness (and meditation, for that matter) isn't for everyone—and for that reason, feel free to skip this section if the thought of these rituals turns you off. Assuming you're still here, though, here's your reward: Mindfulness has profound productivity benefits. And because the practice trains you to focus on the present moment, you will typically earn back the time you spend on it: You'll be able to focus deeper and get distracted far less often.

To practice mindfulness, start by paying attention to all the small actions you do by default with each passing moment. It's kind of fun, in a curious way, to step outside yourself to observe yourself acting out your default intentions with your habit energy. If you found that your intentions were "slippery" in the exercise in the previous chapter, practicing some mindfulness can illustrate why. Our default intentions are fleeting; they are formed one moment to be replaced with a new intention the next, as we encounter new environments that bring forth different conditioned intentions.

Mindfulness can be described as a process of noticing all the intentions we form by default, while at the same time making an effort to draw our attention back to what we're doing when it ventures off to think about the most random of things. It also involves trying not to judge our behavior as we perform actions out of habit energy. (This point might sound random, but judgment is a form of thinking, which prevents us from truly *experiencing* the present moment. Mindfulness is about one thing—noticing what you're experiencing. There's no thinking required.)

It's always helpful to illustrate an idea like this with an example.

Just two minutes ago, to take a short break from writing, I went downstairs to get a snack (a pack of dill pickle crunchy fava beans, if you're curious—though I bet you weren't). Stepping away from my desk and noticing what I was doing in default mode, I automatically slowed down and started acting more slowly. I started by feeling the sensations of the sole of each foot hitting the floor with each consecutive step. In the process, my mind wandered to think about the fact that I should *write* about the fact that I felt each foot hit the floor, but I quickly drew it back to my present-moment intentions—after all, I had a broader intention to practice mindfulness.

Walking down the staircase to the kitchen, I observed all the ways my body automatically choreographed each step, repeatedly transferring weight from one foot to another. (Isn't it great that we don't have to set an intention to take each next step?) Grabbing the last packet of fava beans out of the box, I saw that the box was empty—a cue that then led me to form another default intention, to break down the box to recycle. Seeing a different cue, that the pack of beans was unopened, led me to pull the top off the bag along the rip line and toss the top bit of plastic into the kitchen garbage can.

Noticing my impulse to grab a few beans to eat as I walked up the stairs, I consciously intervened, setting a small, subtle, yet *different* intention to wait until I was upstairs to begin eating them. I wanted to stay mindful, and I didn't want to cram too much into the moment.

These actions sound small, and that's because they are. But in the moment, any action you're fully present with will feel meaningful. That's how attention works. If you take just a bit of time to be aware of yourself following through with your own default intentions, you'll probably notice this same thing, no matter how subtly it may play out. There will invariably come a time when you have the desire to act differently. Then, you'll search within yourself to form an intention that is truer to what you want to do.

Slowing down, you become far more likely to see default intentions arise.

This is the power of noticing your default way of being.

The sum of our default intentions provides us with a default way of living.

Deliberate intention is what we layer on top of this default life, to go our own way, to carve out our own path.

UNLOCKING OUR SELF-REFLECTIVE CAPACITY

Whenever I hit an impasse with something in my work or life, I do something simple: I go for a walk. I have written about the power of mind wandering in my previous books, and so I don't want to step on too much of that same ground here. But it is critical to mention here that there is immense power in letting your mind roam free—wherever it wants to go—when you hit an impasse with something. Sometimes, a fifteen-minute walk produces greater insight than focusing on a problem for several hours.

We tend to store the problems we're facing—and the puzzles we're in the middle of solving—front of mind. When our mind wanders, we think about those problems and puzzles automatically. This makes us more likely to solve them as we poke and prod at them once our mind has a chance to roam free.

When we intentionally let our mind wander—a mental mode I call scatterfocus—our mind likes to wander to some fascinating places.

Think of the last time you took a shower and let your mind run off for a little while. Where did it go? Did you plan your future? Did you come up with ideas?

We come up with an incredible number of both ideas and plans when we scatter our attention. Mostly, we think about the future and our goals. Random sampling studies have found we spend an incredible 48 percent of our time thinking about the future when our mind is wandering.[8] (This percentage is even higher in those who meditate.[9])

We also spend time in the present (28 percent of the time) and the past (12 percent)—recalling memories and thinking about ideas. The remaining 12 percent of the time, we think about other things that cannot be rooted in time, including recalling and connecting ideas. When we bounce among all three mental destinations, we unearth ideas we would never have arrived at otherwise. We automatically think about other people and our relationships more. And, get this: We think about our goals *fourteen times more often* when our mind is wandering compared with when we're focused.[10] Wandering *looks* unproductive, but when done deliberately, it is truly a way we can double down on goal attainment—while solving more problems.

In this wandering, we automatically tap into the volitional sources of intentional action that the monk mentioned—especially our self-reflective capacity.

When you hear the phrase "self-reflective capacity," you likely think of looking inward—like by talking about your day with a friend, journaling about how your day went, or reflecting on your thoughts about a topic. This momentary capacity for reflection is extraordinarily powerful—and so we'll focus on it a lot throughout the book. It's incredibly powerful not just for goal attainment but also for thinking about our goals in the first place. It also helps us solve problems.

If you want to work on autopilot less, become more intentional, and reflect on your future and plan for your goals more often, you need to activate your self-reflective capacity. Whatever that looks like for you, the options are endless: a midday walk to clear your mind, a long bath a few evenings a week, or cooking your favorite meal. Do what you can to get more scatterfocus time.

Focusing on our goals is great—but so is thinking about them more often in the first place.

Throughout the rest of the book, we'll talk about how to form smarter and more deliberate intentions. In the process, we'll connect with our self-reflective capacity, which is critical for goal attainment.

IT'S NOW TIME TO ZOOM out to the values that motivate and drive the intentions we set. This may seem like an odd place to begin in a productivity book. But the research says the opposite: For every intention you set, values are at work behind the scenes, pulling on the strings of what you will do. Understanding them is a key to setting better, stronger intentions.

Let's talk about values.

2

Values

"We do not see things as they are,
we see them as we are."

—*Anaïs Nin*[1]

While your goals determine who you will become, your values tell the story of who you already are.

Values are integral to the process of goal attainment. By setting goals to continually improve your situation (and if you want, yourself), you are able to accomplish more of what you want. And by connecting with who you are, through understanding your values, you can find greater meaning and joy along the way. Most crucial, it is also possible for us to ground our goals in our values, so that they become far more motivating. When a goal is set well, it can even become a part of our identity.

Before we dig into the subject of values, though, I do want to get a disclaimer out of the way first. If you're anything like me, you may not have many (if any) positive associations with the idea of connecting with your values as you enter this chapter. If this is you, I don't blame you one bit—I was the same way.

If you've ever done an exercise to determine what your deepest held values are, you'll know that values can be a somewhat corny topic that at times feels almost made up. For me, before digging into the fascinating science on the topic, the term engendered imagery of the cheesy corporate exercises I had done in the past, where I circled values on a sheet of paper that listed dozens of them. (Most of these exercises aren't based in science.) With this as our starting point, discovering our values may feel a bit like grasping for straws in the dark—choosing random words that *feel* right—generosity! humor! grace!—without truly digging deeper.

Luckily for us all, there is a better way—one that is actually rooted in a wealth of research.

Values are fascinating and worth learning more about. They shine a light on who we really are.

To explore the twelve values from which all others stem, let's zoom out to look at our values from an even higher vantage point.

YOUR MOTIVATIONAL HIERARCHY

We all have our own personal hierarchy of values and see some values as being incredibly important—not ever worth compromising on—while seeing others as ones we can take or leave. Our values serve as a gradient of motivations that propel our actions forward—motivations that vary depending on the broad focus we have in our life.

Researchers define our values as "broad, trans-situational, desirable goals that serve as guiding principles in people's lives."[2] That sentence is worth going back and reading extra slowly once more, because values are a bunch of things all at once. They are:

- **broad**, in that they take place over a long time frame. In fact, values can be thought of as our longest-term intentions or goals;

- **trans-situational**, in that they're always present, behind the scenes, across all the various situations and contexts of our life—whether that's at work, home, the grocery store, or Grandma's house. Wherever you are, whatever you're doing, your values are there with you, making your actions more and less meaningful and motivating, while pulling on the strings of what you will do;

- **desirable**, because they are what we deem most "important and worthy." In fact, we even "see [our] values as closer to [our] ideal self than [with our] personality traits." We also want to change them to a lesser extent. (It's worth noting as well that values are their own distinct construct, independent of traits, motives, and attitudes); and, finally;

- **our guiding principles**, because values underlie and motivate everything we do. We filter both our actions and the actions of others through them.

Simply put, values are our true nature.

In this definition, the word "goals" is also worth touching on. Goals and values are commonly viewed as different things, when in truth our values and goals are much the same. Values *are* goals, but ones that take place across a very long time frame. If you squint your eyes and turn your head a bit, every value is eerily similar to a goal in that it is something we desire to accomplish—only more broadly and over the course of our lives.* Values are our ultimate goals and serve as an articulation of what we are really after in our lives.

Recall another earlier topic, that every one of our actions is connected to one or more of our values—regardless of whether those values are strong for us. Because values are motivational by nature, the higher a value is in our own hierarchy, the more it motivates us to act.[3] Each of our actions has an underlying motivation, and so there is always a value—or multiple values—propelling us forward.

---

*In this same way, every "*intention*" can also be considered a goal—albeit one that is process-focused and of shorter duration. I find it helpful to distinguish between the two topics, as it is helpful to think of our intentions as *expressions* of the goals we have set.

Goals, priorities, values, and intentions are all connected with one another in the Intention Stack—they just differ in their duration, strength, and depth. These connections also tell us something that proves incredibly helpful for goal attainment: With goal setting, values must have a central place if the goal is going to be successful. Goals and intentions that are connected with our values motivate us more and lead us to a greater amount of action—while also making our actions more meaningful to us.

Value-connected goals also complete the picture of the entire Intention Stack. When a goal is aligned and connected with our daily actions *and* our strongest values, we fill out the full picture of a goal. When both of these things are in place, progress toward our goals becomes a change that is both remarkably tangible but also deeply meaningful. Here is the Intention Stack pictured with the twelve fundamental values on top.

The Intention Stack

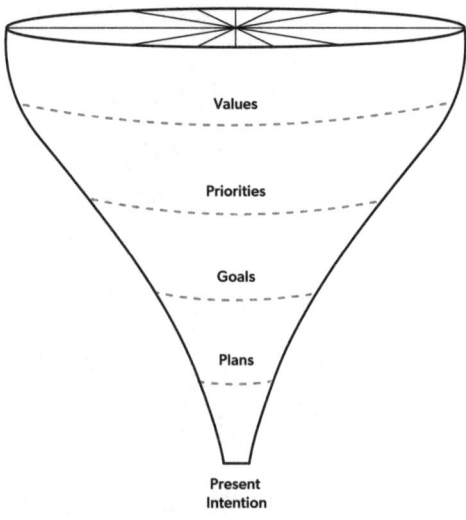

Values

Priorities

Goals

Plans

Present
Intention

When a goal is connected with our values and our daily actions, a goal can be considered completely defined.

PRIORITIES: YOUR SUBVALUES

Our priorities also have a place in the stack, of course, especially in relation to our values. Think of your priorities as an extension of what you value. In essence, priorities are your subvalues that also serve as a container that your goals can fit inside of. Given that the fundamental values represent a motivational continuum, our number of potential priorities is endless. One study, conducted by professors Shalom Schwartz, Sonia Roccas, and Lilach Sagiv, in particular, shows what subvalues can look like. The researchers statistically mapped where certain subvalues fit underneath specific values in the values pie.[4] They found, for example, that the broad value of benevolence can hold priorities that include being helpful, honest, forgiving, loyal, and responsible. On the other side of the pie, the value of achievement can hold priorities that include being successful, capable, ambitious, and influential. Self-direction holds being curious, being free, creative, independent, and choosing your own goals. Countless other priorities can live alongside these when they have the same underlying values motivation.

Just because you value a top-order value—a broader value that your subvalues fit inside of—doesn't mean you'll value every one of the corresponding priorities as well—we all value each top-level value in different amounts.

Some priorities can also be curiously challenging to categorize—including health. For many, health fits inside the value of security because it provides a sense of personal safety. For others, it fits more with hedonism because we can better enjoy our bodies by investing in health. For others still, it fits most squarely inside achievement, because health represents the accomplishment of maintaining optimal wellness. One study on the values of British men and women found that health was connected most with security for men and hedonism for women.

Priorities can be quite subjective. And while there may be a fixed number of values at the top of the Intention Stack, countless priorities (subvalues) get us to them. The best way for you to connect with these is to continually edit your goals to align them with what you value (we'll examine this more in the next chapter). You will connect with many of your priorities along the way.

When it comes to our priorities, optimizing both aversion and desire also helps us make our goals more of a priority in our lives. When a goal is desirable, it connects with our priorities, which connect with our values. We get closer to our priorities with each edited iteration. Taming aversion lets us connect our goals, priorities, and values to the bottom of the Intention Stack—as we act in alignment with our goals daily.

THE FOUR ORIENTATIONS

There are two fundamental polarities that determine our specific top-level values: whether we have a desire to conserve our current state or to try to improve or change things—and whether our focus is on ourselves or others. We all fall somewhere along these two polarities. Where we fall determines which fundamental values we have.

The Four Orientations

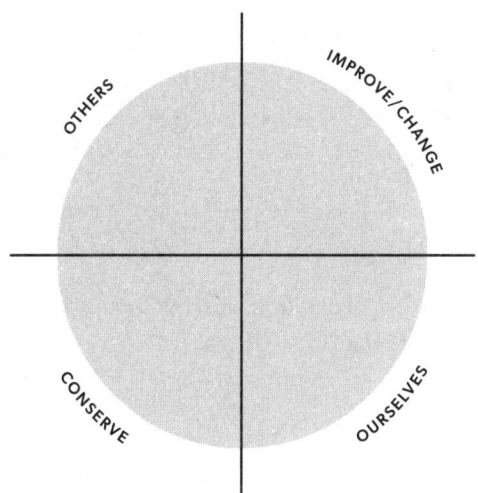

The twelve fundamental values we all share (in different amounts), as first uncovered by professor and researcher Shalom Schwartz, are:

- **Self-direction**: Choosing and cultivating your own thoughts, ideas, and actions

- **Stimulation**: Having novelty, excitement, and challenge in your life

- **Pleasure**: Enjoying hedonistic pleasure, especially through your five senses

- **Achievement**: Attaining success, whether by your own standards or the standards of others

- **Power**: Controlling material resources, social resources, or other people

- **Face**: Preserving your own image and avoiding humiliation

- **Security**: Finding safety and stability both in your environment and in society at large

- **Tradition**: Appreciating, preserving, and maintaining cultural, familial, and religious customs and rituals

- **Conformity**: Abiding by rules, obligations, and expectations while restraining actions that may harm or upset others

- **Humility**: Understanding your insignificance in the grand scheme of things, while believing you are a part of something greater than yourself

- **Universalism**: Understanding, appreciating, and protecting the welfare of people and nature

- **Benevolence**: Being a devoted and reliable member of the groups you are in

Each of these values either fits into one of the polarities or sits on the dividing line between them. To determine your orientations, you can ask yourself the following two questions.

The first: Would I prefer if things stayed the same or would I prefer if they got better?

If, on balance, you want things to stay as they are, you may feel more of a desire to live up to the expectations and obligations others have of you—valuing **conformity**. You may desire stability and safety in your life—valuing **security**. You might also be more inclined to love rituals like gathering with family and friends during holidays—valuing **tradition**. Conversely, if you would generally prefer that things improved across the ways in which you relate to the world, you may instead value thinking for yourself and going your own way—valuing **self-direction**. You are also more likely to enjoy excitement and novelty—valuing **stimulation**.

Of course, our values are not black and white: You likely fall somewhere between these two extremes. Broadly speaking, there is safety, security, and comfort to be found in things remaining predictable; tangible gains and excitement are to be found in things improving for the better. Which of these factors wins out for you is related to which more specific values will be strongest for you.

To determine whether you have an orientation toward others or yourself, ask yourself this second question: Would I prefer to enrich others or to enrich myself?

If you care more about yourself, you may find more meaning in controlling other people or resources—valuing **power**. You may also care more about attaining success by traditional standards and measures—valuing **achievement**. On the other hand, if you care more about enriching others, you may find greater meaning in enhancing the welfare of others—the value of **benevolence**. At the same time, you may also care more about understanding, appreciating, and protecting people and nature—the value of **universalism**.

As with your preference for change, there's also, of course, a lot of middle ground between these two extremes.

That said, there are a few values that don't fall neatly into one of the four orientations. For example, **pleasure**. Curiously, this value can be categorized under both enrichment and openness to change, because pleasure is both self-serving and on some level necessitates that we be open to novel experiences. This is especially true because motivations such as "enjoying life" fall into this broad value, along with more self-indulgent, hedonistic aspects of pleasure. ("Pleasure" is called "hedonism" in the research, but I'll refer to it as both in this book, because depending on the context, some people have associations with the word "hedonism" that don't align with how this value is defined in the research. To me, the word conjures more sultry experiences rather than a fuller spectrum of also-enjoyable sensory experiences—like eating an incredible meal or taking a fancy bath, in addition to the more "sultry" stuff. I'll keep things PG from this point forward.)

In a similar way, **humility** falls into both conserving things as they are and a focus on others. **Face**—maintaining a public image while avoiding humiliation—is similar and fits into both self-improvement and conservation.

THE RELATIVITY OF VALUES

In addition to having orientations, all values exist relative to one another. Some values—like power and achievement—are similar in that they both necessitate a focus on ourselves. Others—like tradition and self-direction, or security and benevolence—are opposing values and contradict each other on a fundamental level.

To help illustrate, in the research done by Shalom H. Schwartz in 1992, values are arranged into a handy pie chart. The more similar two values are, the closer they are to each other in the pie. The less similar, the farther away. For example, humility lives between conformity and universalism in the pie. It's similar in motivation to conformity in that in being humble, we accept our circumstances as they are. Humility and universalism have also been shown to "share a conception of human beings as embedded in a greater reality of which they are but a small part."[5] Similarly, face contains elements of both power and security, and resides smack dab between them. In other words, we feel both powerful and secure when we maintain our image and avoid embarrassment.

Here are the twelve values arranged into this pie hierarchy.*

---

* pierarchry?

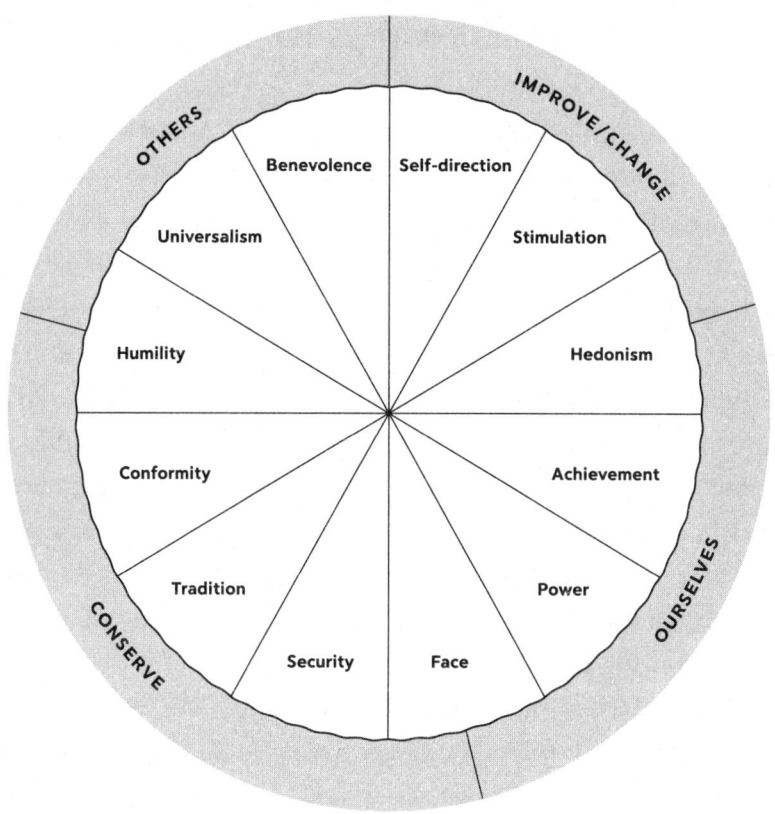

It should come as no surprise that with such basic motivations at its foundation, Schwartz's model stands up across people and across cultures. To date, the circular model has been supported by research on more than three hundred samples in more than eighty countries and has been found to be valid for children as young as five years old. As Schwartz put it, the very structure of our values "suggests that there is a universal organization of human motivations."[6]

FROM TWELVE VALUES TO NINETEEN

When the original theory of human values was published by Schwartz in 1992, it introduced the research world to the fact that human behavior could be categorized by core motivations that live within us all. Since then, the original values have been supported by hundreds of research studies conducted over the ensuing decades, across individuals and cultures. What's emerged is an understanding that it is possible to get more granular and to break down the values even further—increasing their number from twelve to nineteen. (It is worth noting that when the theory of human values was first introduced, it suggested only ten values—later statistical analyses discovered that the values of humility and face were top-level values that had the same force as the original ten; hence, we're talking about the twelve values in this book.)

All the nineteen values are still so-called top-order values, in that they are about as broad as you can get before you begin to drill down to the next level in the values hierarchy. In this book, we won't go much further than this top level, though we will explore how these values filter down into smaller values.

Let's start with the value of self-direction. This value can be broken down into two smaller values: self-directed *thought* and self-directed *action*. In other words, cultivating our own ideas is a different value from determining our own actions. Interestingly, there is also a strong positive association between our level of openness and how self-directed we are—though this openness correlates only with the *thought* component of self-direction.

Security can be broken down into both *societal* security and *personal* security—and in a similar way, you may value one much more than the other. These different values will manifest differently for you, too.

Invincibility Superpowers

One interesting study played around with our security values in a curious way. In it, a team of researchers tried an experiment with a group of participants who identified as more conservative and politically Republican. They then got the participants to each imagine they were in a scenario where they were granted superhero powers. Participants were told they were on a shopping trip when they "wander[ed] into a strange store with no sign out front." In the store, they heard a strange voice that told them that in the morning, they would wake up with a superpower: being "completely invulnerable to physical harm." (The control group's superpower was being able to fly. I'd personally pick being indestructible over flying—participants obviously weren't given a choice.) With their newfound invincibility superpower, participants imagined that knives and bullets bounced right off them, fire didn't burn their skin, and "a fall from a cliff wouldn't hurt at all."

Remarkably, those in the invincibility group felt more physically safe in the experiment. Afterward, they reported being "significantly less socially conservative" with their values. The imaginary scenario did not affect how economically conservative participants were. While the feeling is likely fleeting, it does illustrate a

(continued)

fascinating connection between the value of feeling physically safe and our political attitudes. According to the researchers, feeling safe and secure can even "foster more progressive attitudes."[7] At least temporarily—values are not very malleable over time.

Conformity can also be divided into both *rule-based* and *interpersonal* conformity—either complying with rules, laws, and obligations or avoiding upsetting others. Benevolence can be divided into two types: *caring* for others or being *dependable*. Power can also be expressed in two ways: through exerting *dominance* over other people or control over material or social *resources*. Curiously, the "resource" form of power lives closer to the value of security in the pie—and dominance power lives closer to achievement.

Universalism—understanding and appreciating people and nature—can be divided into three different top-level values, all of which are different ways of expressing the value. First, there's *tolerance*, which is accepting and understanding those who are different from you. Then there's societal *concern*, which is seeking equality and justice for others. And finally, there's preserving and protecting *nature*.

On the following page is the pie, with the twelve values expanded.

The value of health has also been studied for where it might fit into the pie. However, analyses on the subject have proved inconclusive. The location of the value has proven inconsistent across multiple studies, which have identified it as "another value but one whose meaning may vary considerably across cultures." While health may be something you value in spades, it is likely a subvalue to one of your original twelve—or, if you'd prefer, nineteen.

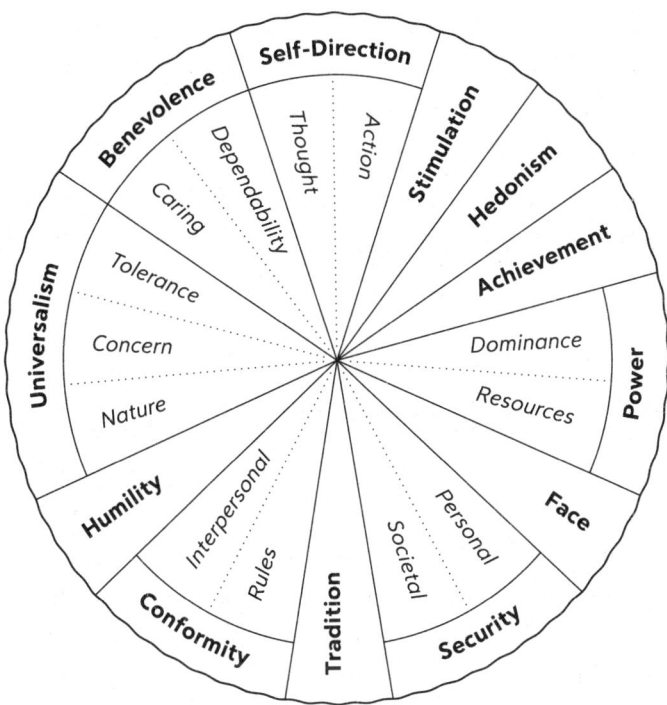

One other value not included in the pie is happiness. As you might have guessed, it is absent for a reason. As Schwartz has written, "Although happiness is an important value, it is not included because [we] achieve it through attaining whatever outcomes [we] value."[8, 9]

Just as with success, happiness comes from living through our values, and so it is separate from the pie.

THE BUILDING BLOCKS OF VALUES

Some values will be strong for you because you were conditioned that way by your biology and previous experiences, while others will be strong for you because your previous intentional actions have solidi-fied into your default intentions, which have formed your character.

To see where your values come from, look to your default inten-tions and habits.

According to a fascinating research review titled "Personal Values in Human Life," published in the renowned journal *Nature Human Behaviour* by professors Lilach Sagiv, Sonia Roccas, Jan Cieciuch, and Shalom Schwartz, our values come from the same familiar places that our default intentions do: our genetics and the social environments we find ourselves in—time with family, while at school, or with our community and society at large. Interestingly, the researchers write that "no unifying model has been proposed that integrates these factors"—though in looking through the study, it is difficult not to see how our default intentions inform the values we have. There is near complete overlap between where our default intentions and our values come from. This makes sense, given our default intentions drive so much of what we do—and the theory of human values is essentially a motiva-tional continuum of why we act the way we do.[10]

From an early age, we are conditioned by people and circumstances to respond in a certain way to events and to have certain default in-tentions. When you zoom out from this, you can see that it tends to be broadly oriented in the ways we've talked about in this chapter—toward enriching others or enriching ourselves, or conserving things or making them better. At the same time, this conditioning can be categorized into more certain broader priorities as well. For example, we might learn to go our own way (self-direction), help others (benevolence), and live up to our full potential (achievement). These default intentions be-come the raw material that we construct our broader values out of.

Our values are the sum of our defaults.

The more we reflect on our actions, the more often we can decide to form intentions that are different from the conditioned ones we have by default. This is the process through which we shape how our values develop. The more expansive our self-reflective capacity, the more actively we participate in shaping the person we become.

Our deliberate intentions also, at some point, become so routine that they dissolve into the foundation of who we are. This is why, as James Clear has written in *Atomic Habits*, we must see the habits we are trying to form as a part of our identity. With enough repetition, our deliberate intentions become our defaults. This is the ground that we stand on in our daily life; this is the ground on which we can practice other deliberate intentions. These deliberate intentions, of course, allow us to make room for change.

It's no wonder why the monk argued that it is the sum of our intentions that determines who we are as a human being.

WHERE OUR VALUES COME FROM

Research shows that our parents and caregivers are the primary source of our values—which makes sense when you consider the influential role our parental figures have in shaping our default intentions and the person we become. Social norms and contagion (which are the traits and habits we pick up from others) are a strong force: Those in a parental role transmit values to us both directly (e.g., by guiding us through what to do) and indirectly (e.g., by modeling their own values through their actions, which we then see as an example for ourselves).[11] We learn from our siblings, too.

When you look at your parents and then look at yourself, you can see that you obviously aren't like them in every way—maybe even in some ways you're grateful about. You've probably taken some of the good while leaving some of the bad. Research shows that we have an active role in the process of defining our own values and get to "choose to adopt or reject the values [we] perceive" that our parents have.[12] The more connected we feel with our parents in general, the more similar our values tend to be. In addition, the greater our self-reflective capacity, the more active participants we tend to be in defining our values as well—we simply reflect more often on what we would like to do and where we would like to go.

Not all our value conditioning comes from our parents, of course. Many of our values come from the social environments we find ourselves in over the course of our lives. For starters, we typically share the same socioeconomic status as our parents. This means we hang around many of the same places, which also happen to have the same types of school districts, the same level of safety, and the same culture. Each experience that conditions us across all these contexts fits into one or more of the twelve basic values.

Every action we will ever take has an underlying motivation that propelled us to act in the first place. Behind each of our default intentions is a fundamental human value. **The sum of the motivations behind our default intentions determines our values.** We see our actions as more meaningful when they are connected to the ways in which we have learned and decided to act in the past.

Along the way, as when we choose from among the values of our parents, we take an active role in shaping the person we are becoming through whatever self-reflective capacity we have developed.

While we are all unique in what we value, it is worth pointing out that there are some commonalities a lot of us share. According to research, "Values are a core element of culture."[13] After all, they are constructed out of our collective intentions and actions. They are a representation of the goals we all seek.

Many of our values help us serve others. For example, it is through exercising conformity that we restrain any of our actions that may be socially disruptive, and through our value of benevolence that we all help the groups we are members of to flourish. Collaboration is evolutionarily adaptive: It is through working together with others that we make the groups we are a member of stronger.

One study examined the values people had across sixty-three societies and found that overall, self-direction and benevolence tended to top the list of what people valued. Most of us are members of societal groups—like families, educational systems, communities, as well as society at large—and these two values help us to support the groups we are a part of. This should make you feel good: Research has found that "values that express a motivation to care for close others are among the most important values to most people in most societies."[14]

For example, through the value of benevolence we consider and cooperate with others, which protects the stability (and security) of our societal groups. Self-direction, meanwhile, motivates us to independently come up with novel ideas and solutions that can benefit the groups we're a part of. Both of these functions are critical. Just as we may or may not value conserving things versus improving things, research has found that "groups require both stability and plasticity in order to survive."[15]

A FEW MORE THINGS YOUR VALUES SAY ABOUT YOU

So far in this chapter we have established what values are, where they come from, and why they're important. We've also broken down how the various top-level values are related to one another. Before we begin to get tactical, though, let's dig into a few ways our values predict our actions and beliefs. It's kind of wild the extent to which our values predict our behavior—though it should not be surprising, given that our values are made up of our default intentions.

Let's start with what the research says about our values and religion (which is, of course, a subject with no controversy whatsoever). As you might guess, religiosity is positively associated with some values and negatively associated with others. The value of tradition is usually especially strong with those who are religious, as are the more conservative values of conformity and security. Opposite values to these—such as pleasure, self-direction, and stimulation—are *negatively* associated with being religious. As Sagiv, Roccas, Cieciuch, and Schwartz posit in their great *Nature Human Behaviour* review, which I've referenced throughout this chapter, "Hedonism is particularly incompatible with religiosity because a primary function of all religions is to temper self-indulgence and gratification of material desires." When we develop default intentions related to religion, the motivation behind these intentions tends to involve tradition in some way. It is worth noting that these associations held true across twenty-one samples in fifteen countries, with tradition being most highly correlated with being religious, and hedonism most negatively correlated.

Career choice is another area heavily related to our values. For example, research has shown that those of us who value benevolence and universalism are more likely to become psychologists and social workers; those who value security, conformity, and tradition are more likely to become secretaries and accountants; and those of us who value power and achievement are significantly more likely to become managers, bankers, and financial advisers. It's tough to determine, between our values and default intentions, which is the chicken and which is the egg when it comes to what influences our career choice most. Correlation does not mean causation. Either way, the more of a fit our values are with our career, the more satisfied we will be at work.

This idea proves true across other contexts in our life as well, of course. The more aligned our actions are with our values in general, the more meaningful, important, and worthwhile our actions tend to feel. We'll be more motivated to follow through with them as well.

Research has also found that our values predict our everyday actions and how we relate to others.* The more we value benevolence, the more likely we are to volunteer to help others, donate money to social causes, and see being a volunteer as a part of our identity. Additionally, valuing universalism has been shown to make us more tolerant of minority members of a group or society when we are a part of the dominant group—a correlation that is maintained across cultures.

Our individual values also hold up remarkably well over *time*. This shouldn't be a surprise. Because our values describe the architecture of our default intentions, changing a value requires undoing a lot of conditioning—or creating a lot of new conditioning to balance out a new value with the original opposing one. It's no surprise then, as researchers have phrased it, that "the extent of consistency in values across time is remarkable."[16] But with that said, sometimes our values do shift—particularly when we find ourselves in new environments that

---

*This extends also to disagreements we have with others, which are often an expression—or clash—of different values. If you believe in an issue to your core, your values are probably at play behind the scenes. For example, differing opinions on immigration can be seen as a conflict between universalism and security and tradition. Just as differing opinions on climate change can be seen as universalism pitted against power, particularly in the context of economic power and control. I should say that I am not an expert on these issues and write about them here with quite a lot of trepidation, but it is worth offering them up as food for thought. I personally find it easier to connect with those I disagree with when I can see their differing values at play behind the scenes. I can more easily empathize with where they're coming from, even if I find their viewpoints hard personally to relate to.

we must adapt to. To take a more dramatic example, this is especially the case when we move to a new country, when we find ourselves in a new place that offers us a new set of socially contagious default intentions.

Two studies looked at people who emigrated from Russia to Finland, and from Poland to the United Kingdom. Those who immigrated to Finland developed stronger values with universalism and security. Those who moved to the UK had self-direction and power values that shifted to become more in line with those who lived in the new country. And both found that participants' values continued to shift over time, as they had more time to settle in.

Though our values can shift over time, it obviously takes an incredible amount of time and effort to change what we value. Generally, we must accumulate new default intentions that are in line with where we wish to go. If you've ever tried to adopt a new habit, you'll know how difficult changing one small behavior can be.

Now imagine trying to change the entire foundation of who you are.

This was a lesson that I had to learn the hard way with my value of pleasure/hedonism—a story I'll share in chapter 6, where we'll get more tactical with our values and goals.

TWO WAYS TO CALCULATE YOUR VALUES

While reading this chapter, you've probably developed an intuitive sense for what your strongest values are. In this section, I'll give you a couple ways to calculate your values, before we get tactical with them.

The first way is a simple activity you can do without having to take a values questionnaire. The other is a more comprehensive test to determine the values you hold most dear.

The easiest, most time-efficient but somewhat less accurate way to determine your strongest and weakest values is to start with a list of values and sort them by which ones connect with you the most. I recommend doing this activity slowly, with the definitions of the values in front of you, so you can really process and reflect on them. Rank the values from highest to lowest, according to which ones speak to you on a deeper level. Your top values will feel almost instinctive—core principles you will not want to compromise. Then, there will be your middling values. And finally, the values you either are repelled by or don't care much about.

If it's hard to rank them by instinct, try to **order the values based on where you spend your time**. How you spend your time and resources is indicative of which values you likely have. Because values relate to our default intentions and our deliberate intentions, looking back at how you spent your time during the last month or more will give you a pretty good indication of which values you engage with most often on a daily basis.

Don't worry about getting things exact—you can always revise the order later. But do make sure to really consider what your strongest and weakest three values are.

This test is more subjective than it is scientific, but it will give you a loose approximation of what you instinctively value the most.

If you want to get more granular, scientific, and accurate, you can also take a comprehensive values test. Because a values test would be too long for this book, I posted one to the book's website, at chrisbailey .com/intentional. This test has to live online for a couple reasons. First, it's a long test, and scoring for it is a bit complicated. Second, and more important, I very unfortunately have to pay a licensing fee each time the test is taken, so taking the test has to cost a small fee (or else I would lose a fortune). Please believe me: It bugs me that this has to cost money. I personally believe a test like this should be free—and maybe by the time you read these words, I will have found a way to accomplish this. Fortunately, the test is based on the most scientifically validated instrument for measuring our values, the Revised Portrait Value Questionnaire (PVQ-RR). I think the small fee is worth it. But the methods above for uncovering your largest values will also do the trick if you don't feel inclined to go that deep!

Either way, our values can be thought of as the truest possible articulation of who we are.

They're worth connecting with.

MY TOP VALUES

So far we've discussed values from a mostly theoretical level. To give you an example of how our values connect with our everyday reality, let me share which ones are at the top and bottom of my own list, while connecting these to my own daily life.

By this point in the book, you probably have some idea of which values are strongest and weakest for you—there are probably a select few values that you feel at your core and others you find incredibly aversive to even think about. There will also be some that you feel kind of *meh* about. I felt all this while I was looking through the research. Curious to dig more into my own values, I took the PVQ-RR test based on the theory of fundamental human values to discover what my strongest and weakest values are.

If you're curious, here are all my own values, ordered from strongest to weakest:

- Self-direction (by a wide margin)

- Pleasure/Hedonism

- Humility

- Universalism

- Security

- Face

- Conformity

- Benevolence

- Achievement

- Stimulation

- Tradition

- Power

Seeing my results, essentially nothing surprised me—it all just felt right. In fact, it confirmed and articulated a lot of what I had intuitively felt about myself. Looking at my top three values, I value self-direction incredibly highly, arguably sometimes to a fault. A surefire way to get me *not* to do something is to tell me that I *have to* do it. I also strongly value sensory pleasure—my second top value. On this note, I remember pretty much every meal I've ever eaten at a restaurant. I can also luxuriate in the sound of my favorite songs for hours and find taking baths when traveling a guaranteed way to relax. (Baths are polarizing, but I'd wager there's a connection between how much we enjoy them, and how much we value pleasure and how little we value stimulation.) Humility is also incredibly important to me—even if it's a value I find awkward to write about. It deeply bothers me when someone who is in a "lucky" position isn't grateful for what they have, or when they don't treat others with respect and kindness. Universalism is also near the top of my list: I find that there is a remarkable beauty to be found in other people and in nature, and find I typically make an active effort to understand people who are different from myself. When someone is different from me, I automatically perk up a bit and get curious, rather than feeling frustrated that they're not like me.

The values near the bottom of my list are informative, albeit in a different way. Power is by far my lowest-ranked value. I have zero desire to have power or dominance over any other person, ever. (It's no wonder power and humility are near opposites of each other in the values pie.) I'm one of the least competitive people you'll ever meet— I'd rather lose a board game than have to compete intensely in one. (Cribbage is about as competitive as I get, and that game is mostly luck.) Also, one of my biggest pet peeves is when someone is rude to waiters or other servicepeople in a restaurant, when for some reason they see themselves as being above them and can't simply be nice. (As a long-ago restaurant waiter, I could go on about this, but I'll spare you the rant!) As you can see, we often have a visceral reaction to the values others do and do not have.

Moving up the list, I can mostly do without tradition—though I do love gathering with people I love and I get a lot of pleasure out of celebrating holidays when everyone's together (especially when there's good food involved). Stimulation is also near the bottom for me— and probably describes why my preferred ways of finding pleasure are more on the relaxing side of the spectrum (baths) rather than on the stimulating end (nights out shouting over music at the bar).

If you have a close friend, partner, colleague, or someone else with whom you have a close relationship, I highly recommend doing the short values test with them, to compare your results. Doing this won't just illuminate your own values—it'll also shine a light on your relationship in some fascinating ways.

While I was doing research for this book, my wife took the test so we could compare notes and use the results to be more intentional about our own relationship. We both value universalism—it's her highest value by a wide margin—along with self-direction. This also explains her choice of career: She's a professor and development economist who has devoted most of her life to helping others, which is, in a large way, a combination of these two values. But we do differ in other equally curious ways. For example, she values stimulation a lot more highly than I do. While I'd prefer to make about one plan a week, she'd prefer to make exciting plans multiple times a week. (I love seeing friends, but as you already know, I also like lying on the couch and ordering takeout.) Realizing this, we make sure we make time to try things together, but she also readily makes plans with friends or goes on adventures on her own when she knows I'm at my limit. I like to relax on vacations (read: do basically nothing), while she likes to "travel"—seeing the sights and adventuring all day. Seeing this difference a while back helped us find a happy middle ground: She runs or cycles through a city in the morning to explore and scope out things to do or try, then we visit one of these things together later in the day.

Pay special attention to where you're most similar and most different. Your actions may make a lot more sense through the lens of what you both value.

A NEW DEFINITION OF SUCCESS

More than twenty years ago—that sentence fragment hurt to write—I got inspired to run a marathon. Curious to discover more about running one, I pored over all the books I could find about the topic, devouring and learning what I could. I learned about breathing techniques, how a training schedule can intensify over time, and how to maintain a certain pace. Over the ensuing months, I built up my endurance to the point where I could run for hours on end. On bad-weather days, I remember having enough time to watch two full movies while running on the treadmill indoors.

So, with the full length of a marathon easily in my sights, I did what most people probably wouldn't: I stopped training entirely.

I didn't give up. At that point, feeling as though I *could* have run one was more than enough for me. If you value achievement, you are probably feeling completely baffled by this sentiment. But as far as my values were concerned, my work was done—and I felt happy with what I had accomplished. Wiping my hands clean of the goal, satisfied, I went on with my life.

Over the ensuing years, I've also thought back to this with a bit of confusion. Why did it make so much sense for me to stop, when I was so close to achieving something big that I had put a lot of effort into? I never once regretted the decision. But I wanted to understand it.

In thinking about this goal through the lens of values, the decision makes a lot more sense. It may not make sense to you if you don't value self-direction as much as I do, but to me it was the training itself that was meaningful. Especially in the build-up stage, when I could feel myself making progress. It was an exercise in going my own way to discover more about a process that I was curious about, while investing in my health. I also got a lot of pleasure from the running itself—especially with how I felt riding a runner's high during and after a long running session. That hedonistic pleasure was meaningful, too. (I enjoyed the calmer feeling after the run more than the high during the run itself—this may be reflective of my stimulation value.)

If you happen to be someone who values accomplishment, at least more than I do, you may feel frustrated by the story. Maybe you're thinking, *Why didn't he just run the thing? He was so close! He'll never be that young and spritely again—there's no way he can run a marathon today; twenty years was so long ago! He's so old now!* Jokes aside, though, I honestly felt fulfilled. I had learned about the topic in a self-directed way and knew I could run a marathon if I wanted to. The whole process was fun. That was the meaningful part to me.

As the book goes on, we'll spend a good amount of time talking about completing the Intention Stack by aligning our plans and goals with what we value. What you'll realize is that by chasing your values instead of chasing success, you unexpectedly obtain even more success, even by traditional measures. After all, your actions will prove more naturally motivating to you, and you'll be more inclined to want to make progress. When work is naturally motivating, productivity comes easily.

Even if you *don't* achieve as much success by traditional measures (money, status, or recognition—or running a marathon after training for it for months, for example), the ironic thing is you'll ultimately *feel* more successful and fulfilled because you will have lived a life in alignment with your values. **At the end of the day, this is what success really is: being true to who we are on a fundamental level.** The truer we are to ourselves, the more successful we feel—and in my view, the more successful we become.

If you value accomplishment, and you achieve great things, you will feel successful. Just as if you value universalism and help a great number of people, you'll feel successful. Just as if you value tradition and live a rich and fulfilling life at home, you'll feel successful.

The only yardstick we should be using to measure our success is how well we live up to what we value most.

At the beginning of the book, I shared the story of the many goals that I've dropped in the past. If you're like me and you don't value accomplishment as much as other people do, you may find that you have goals that are much like my goal of running a marathon—things you could have achieved but didn't. (If you value accomplishment, you may not have as many!)

Maybe there's the promotion you *could* have worked ridiculously hard for that could have set you up to afford a bigger house and live a more lavish life. Maybe your colleagues thought the job was yours for the taking, but at the end of the day, you wanted to spend more time with your family instead. Your universalism and benevolence values won out over your value of achievement. Or maybe there's a goal—writing a book, learning a new skill, or running a marathon—that you keep meaning to take action toward that for some reason you can never quite muster the motivation for.

There's no need to feel guilty for achieving things you don't truly want, that would serve only your achievement value while serving few of the others. At the risk of sounding corny, we all get one short life, within which we have only so much time to spend in a way that fills us with meaning and happiness. Research tells us that some of us are not inspired by achieving things simply for the sake of having achieved them. That's okay.

Just because you don't value achievement highly doesn't mean that you won't achieve anything that is meaningful for you or the groups you're a part of. Chances are you'll actually achieve things that are *more* meaningful to you—not for the sake of success but for reasons that connect to your deeper values. To pick three, maybe you seek to help others because that connects with your value of universalism. Maybe through fueling this value, you decide to become the founder of a charity with a presence in thirty countries. Maybe, to find fuel through connecting with your benevolence value, you provide foster care for more than seventy-five kids in order to give them an incredible start in life. (As my mom's mom did through her incredible life of serving others.) By constantly being on the lookout for opportunities that fuel your stimulation value, you may seek out projects that make a bigger and bigger difference—to keep the excitement going—and along the way become a world-leading expert in your field.

If you don't value achievement, achieving things for the sake of achieving them will feel like a hollow pursuit. But the opposite also holds true if you *do* value accomplishment. If you enjoy striving for great things, whether to challenge yourself or push yourself to your full potential, you'll in all likelihood discover great joy in the pursuit of accomplishment. This will prove especially true as you pursue your other values at the same time. Consider working toward the same definition of success—and to do so, don't just stop with your value of accomplishment.

The curious thing about our values is that we never value only one thing. While some of your values will prove to be stronger than others, the most meaningful actions we can take are those that satisfy multiple values at once. Some people I know highly value achievement— while also valuing universalism and protecting other people and the planet. The more of a difference they make in (and for) the world, the more accomplished they feel—they can derive incredible joy from connecting with the two values at the same time. Others that I know value things like accomplishment and benevolence—and find the greatest amount of meaning in helping and fighting for others. Others value both accomplishment and tradition, and discover the greatest amount of joy in supporting their kids in realizing their full potential.

Regardless of our top values, it is through not just investing in one of our values but multiple values at the same time that we find the greatest meaning in what we pursue.

It's worth reflecting on why you wish to become more productive and follow through on your goals more often. In all likelihood, as with the other goals you have, the reason is probably your values.

When we seek productivity for the right reasons, our actions automatically become both more motivating and meaningful. After all, they're aligned with who we are. This is not always possible, but over time, it's worth fighting to shape your work so that it's more meaningful to you.

Meaning is made when we manifest our values through our actions—across every context of our life.

3

Goal Editing

Let's now move down the Intention Stack to talk about goals.

If intentionality is the key to finishing what we start, goals are how we get there. They are the vehicle through which we accomplish what we set out to do, as much as they are also the end result.

To have the best chance at following through on your goals, you have to know how to structure them well. This means knowing your desired outcome, identifying what you need to do in order to make progress, then continuously keeping tabs on that progress. But, perhaps most important, it also means knowing how to adjust as you go—and when it's time to quit and move on to something else.

Specific goals can be surprisingly difficult to truly define and articulate—this is what makes editing the ones we set necessary. This way, we can make iterative edits to how we plan to improve, so that over time we move toward what we're truly after.

Sometimes when we set a goal, we become fixated on some end result that doesn't hold much weight in reality. Take losing weight as an example. When I started on my goal to lose fat, my initial goal was to drop fifteen pounds. Over time, though, I realized this amount was more a nice round number than anything else. Learning my way through the process, I redefined the goal constantly. In the process, I zeroed in on what I was really after: more of a calorie balance in my life—but while enjoying plenty of good food along the way. Eventually, my goal became more about how I could balance my two values of health (with a calorie balance) and hedonism (with delicious food). It can take quite a few edits to whittle down to the goal we are truly after.

When we arrive at the finish line—the end of the timeline of goal attainment—we will have made enough progress, and moved enough in the right direction, to attain the goal we set and refined. This end point looks different depending on the goal. Maybe we look in the mirror and feel healthy and strong in our body. Or we lie on the couch one evening, feeling deeply fulfilled because of the relationships in our life. Or we earn enough money through our side hustle to make the bills balance at the end of the month and feel secure.

Wherever we wish to go, goals and intentions get us there.

So often, though, we go about setting goals the wrong way.

BEYOND SMART GOALS

Before getting into the ideas in this chapter, I want to address a very popular goal-setting strategy that has been floating around the productivity ether for quite a while: setting SMART goals. I find this model a good illustration for what the activities in this chapter *don't* include. Simply put, certain features of goals are not worth expanding on—for reasons supported by research.

While the SMART acronym goes by different abbreviations, in general, the method states that our goals should be:

- **S**pecific,

- **M**easurable,

- **A**chievable,

- **R**ealistic, and

- **T**ime-bound.

Before sharing what the research on SMART goals says, I should say that I expected this idea would be a shoo-in for the book. The SMART acronym is catchy, memorable, and feels like it should work. It's also immensely practical: Every letter of the method is essentially a step for defining and understanding your goals. There's a reason the idea has traveled so far. But the rule's origin is a bit similar to the rule that says we should get ten thousand steps every day, which originated in a marketing campaign for a Japanese product that counted our daily steps. The number was nice and round, and it made intuitive sense. It took off—but it wasn't necessarily supported by science.

SMART goals originated from a 1981 article written by a business consultant that was published in a magazine named *Management Review*. The rule was designed to support "management excellence." The acronym originally stood for Specific, Measurable, Assignable (we "should specify who will do" the goal), Realistic, and Time-related. It has since been reshaped through a cultural game of telephone.[2]

The article cited no research. It also wasn't rooted in any goal-setting theory. Yet the rule was simple, mnemonic, and made intuitive sense. It quickly took off.

I don't want to mention the name of the original article's author in this book, especially because I'm about to throw their SMART goals idea under the bus. And they deserve some slack here: When they wrote the 965-word piece in 1981, they likely didn't expect that it would go as "viral" as it did. They presumably also wrote it with the best of intentions, to help managers lead higher-performing teams.

Unfortunately, the research verdict is in: The rule is simply not helpful. In some cases, it can even be downright *counter*productive.

One narrative review, published in the *Health Psychology Review*, went so far as to highlight how "there is a risk of *research waste* where funding is awarded to research based on SMART goals" because of how ineffective they are.[3] The paper, which examined research on whether the SMART method helps with attaining physical activity goals, warned that there are a number of reasons why this criticism is true.

For starters, the method isn't based in science. To date, there have been thousands of studies published on the psychology of goal attainment. The SMART acronym is unfortunately not only not supported by this research, it often contradicts it. For example, research recommends that we set challenging, difficult goals—this makes us more likely to achieve more. The SMART acronym does the opposite by focusing on goals that are instead Achievable and Realistic. In other words, we make less progress than we would through other goal-setting methods. Our goals should be as challenging as our resources allow for.

Goals also don't always need to be Specific to be effective. This is especially the case when we're in the learning stage of goal achievement. Researchers Edwin Locke and Gary Latham make the helpful distinction between "learning goals," where we're acquiring a new skill or discovering something new, and "performance goals," where we have a skill that we're employing to execute the goal. They have found that when "in the early stages of learning a new, complex task," "trying for specific, challenging goals may actually *hurt* performance" (*emphasis* mine).[4]

The published review also calls into question just how necessary all the criteria in the model are. For example, aren't Measurable goals also already Specific? Aren't Realistic and Achievable goals pretty much the same thing?

While SMART goals sound good on the surface—great, even—they don't hold water in practice. They're not based on research or evidence, don't consider what kind of goal you're setting, are redundant in their criteria, and likely also aren't being used as they were originally intended—as a goal-setting technique for managers.

Defining SMART goals is a lot better than doing nothing—the simple act of thinking through our goals makes us more likely to achieve them, regardless of whether the method we use to do so is optimal or effective. But there are far better strategies for defining your goals and thinking through how you'll accomplish them.

THE REASON YOU'RE NOT FOLLOWING THROUGH ON YOUR GOALS

Before we jump too deep into this chapter, I want to confess something: I've never really set big, traditional goals for myself.

By "big, traditional goals," I'm referring to outcome-based goals where we try to achieve something grand and specific. I've personally never had goals like hitting grandiose book sales milestones, outsourcing my entire life, or being the first productivity expert on the moon. I work hard, plan, and strategize to the best of my ability, but in the last decade of researching and exploring the topic of personal productivity, I have never been convinced that there is a lot of value in setting goals to achieve big, audacious things. I find there's far more value in focusing on the process, instead of the end result.

My reason for this has always been simple: We do not have complete control over what we accomplish. We can control our efforts and actions—which are the inputs that lead to whatever outcomes we will inevitably reach. But it is impossible to control the outcomes themselves. The reality is more nuanced: The best we can hope to do is try to predict the results of our efforts.

It is in this way that **every goal you set is ultimately a prediction— a guess at where you believe your current and planned actions will take you**.

Sometimes your future will be easy enough to predict. If you set aside $1,000 every month for a year, by the end of a year you'll have saved $12,000. But sometimes your spouse will come down with a bad flu and your hot-water heater will burst all over the basement floor—and because of the expensive fray that is your daily life, you won't be able to put aside enough money to reach your goal.

This is par for the course: Life is complex. In setting goals for the future, it is impossible to account for this complexity.

This is not a bad thing—it's just the reality we must consider for how we set and think about goals. No matter how hard or intelligently you work, things will rarely go as you expect them to. So much of what you expect will go wrong won't. And when things go wrong, they'll often go wrong in a way that didn't even occur to you! We still very much have control over our current intentions and actions, which lead us closer to where we would like to go. But you should know, a lot of the intentions you will make about the actions you will take will be wrong. Predicting the future is almost impossible to do, especially when there is human behavior involved.

Funny enough, these same misplaced expectations about the predictability of our goals can also lead us to greater impatience. We expect that tasks will require less time than they ultimately need, and so we rush through them, propelled forward by a rolling frustration that things are "taking too long." These feelings of impatience arise in the moment, but this same frustration manifests across longer timescales. Sometimes we set ourselves up for disappointment when we don't achieve the things we expect we will—even when we still accomplish great and meaningful (but different) things. Other times, in hyperfocusing on our goals, we miss out on better and more interesting opportunities, as we become fixated on a goal that is less meaningful than we originally thought.

Focus Hours

While your daily capacity for accomplishment can be frustratingly difficult to estimate, **keep in mind that you have about four focused hours in you each workday.** Your capacity to focus each day is limited— and focusing on complex things all day long can be a recipe for exhaustion after a while. While we're all different, and we all do different types of work, generally speaking, we have around four focused hours in us every day. For this reason, I'll typically limit my daily "deep work" time to four or four and a half hours (including during my time blocks, chapter 7)—doing admin work and less cognitively intense work outside of that time. This way, I can respect my daily focus limit and make sure my productivity level stays

(continued)

> sustainable in the long run—while ensuring ample time for simpler tasks and breaks in between. Running past this can compromise our productivity both in the short and long run.

Instead of focusing on goals that are really just predictions or expectations in disguise, our attention is better invested elsewhere: in what leads us closer to the very outcomes we're trying to predict. Instead of getting frustrated, we should focus on our inputs, while seeing every goal as what it really is: a prediction. By choosing to focus on inputs instead of outcomes, we invest our energy into what leads to greater accomplishment over the longer arc of time—while we work, to the best of our ability, to make incremental improvements over time.

The trick, along the way, is not to let the predictions you make turn into expectations about how things will go.

STRUCTURING GOOD GOALS

Setting good goals need not be incredibly complicated. In most cases, it's better if you're left with more time to both make progress and reflect on the progress you're already making—and make necessary changes along the way.

To start, there are three components that each of your goals should have:

1. The outcome you predict your efforts will lead you to (e.g., to save enough money for a house down payment).

2. The process or processes that will lead you to achieving this outcome (e.g., to put 5 percent of every paycheck into your house savings account).

3. The rate at which you are making progress (e.g., to have enough for the down payment in three years).

Our outcome goals are what we "bite off" in order to make some progress in the right direction, while process goals are the steps we will take to get there. On the Intention Stack, these goals are located somewhere in the middle, between our values and daily actions. Outcomes exist higher up, because they're less tangible—more of an idea we can get behind than a next action for us to take. Here are both, plotted on the Intention Stack.

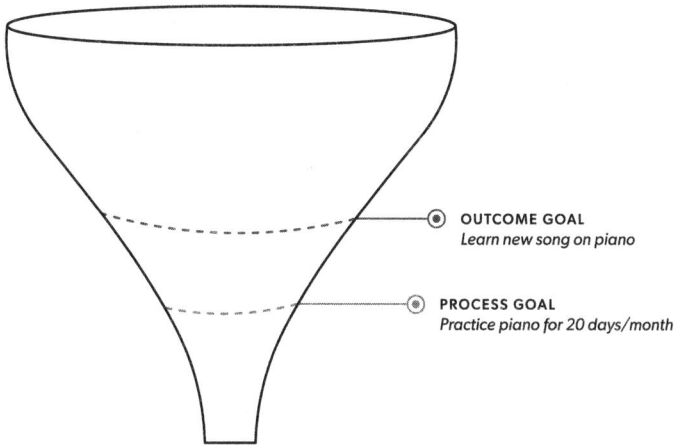

OUTCOME GOAL
Learn new song on piano

PROCESS GOAL
Practice piano for 20 days/month

Let's dive into both types of goals, after which we'll discuss our rates of progress.

Outcome and Process Goals

I already shared how I'm not a big fan of outcome-based goals, which are goals to achieve a specific thing. But I admittedly overstated their lack of usefulness in order to make a point. The truth is, as it often is, more nuanced.

Outcome goals are quite useful for motivating us. They also connect us with a greater purpose while helping us to think through what is required of us to achieve them.

In contrast to outcome goals, a process goal is a goal that is also a plan of action—like building a morning running ritual, meditating for at least five minutes a day, or writing a thousand words a week for a year.

As you might imagine, process goals and outcome goals are intrinsically interconnected. After all, every process goal leads us to a certain outcome. That's why we do them! Together, both types of goals determine how quickly we will make progress toward the outcomes we are predicting.

The research supports how both types of goals are helpful, yet serve different purposes. One study found, for example, that while process goals motivate us more into *acting* toward our goals, outcome goals lead to better *results* overall. If you're like me, and you have an aversion to setting either type of goal, this aversion may be misplaced.

Both serve a purpose, and can often be thought of as two sides of the same coin.[5]

Outcome-based goals are worth defining because while we might not be able to control the broader outcomes in our life, the outcomes we're striving for are still worth *predicting*. Outcomes are powerful because they give our process goals something to fit inside of—a broader goal that becomes a story of change that motivates us and that we feel inspired to make a reality.

Outcome goals get us excited in a way that process goals don't. "Live a fabulously wealthy life in retirement" is likely far more motivating for you than "save 20 or 25 percent of my gross yearly income." Just as "have eight-pack abs for beach season" is more motivating than "eat only kidney beans and cucumbers for nine straight months." (I haven't road tested this strategy. It sounds like a bad idea.)

If you're crafting a goal, it's important not to leave any motivation on the table—especially given that the motivation you have at the inception of a goal is likely to wane over time. Predicting the outcomes that your actions will lead to helps you do this. Constructed correctly, outcome-focused goals can light a fire underneath you. Just be sure to revise your predictions (edit them) regularly.

This is something I found out firsthand when I looked at my own goals. While I had been averse to setting outcome goals, after exploring the science behind them, I decided to create a corresponding outcome goal for each of the process goals I was investing in. For example, my process goal to keep a certain amount of money in my company was suddenly connected to an outcome goal to "operate a sustainable business." Similarly, my goal to "invest in a Couch to 10K program" was connected to one to "rebuild my cardiovascular system" after I had surgery. (I'm okay!) Predicting the outcome my process goals led me to required very little extra time—and I found I more than made this time back in how much additional motivation I had to achieve my goals.

My interest in daily productivity (and perhaps middling accomplishment value) no doubt led me to focus more on the bottom of the Intention Stack—where our daily actions live. But it's important that we consider the more substantial outcomes our actions will lead us to as well. These outcomes give our goals meaning and depth. Even if, at the end of the day, they prove to be more predictions than the reality that we are in the middle of creating. (Luckily, all these variables are easy to revise.)

In addition to defining outcome-based goals, process goals are worth defining, too.

A process goal is the next step—or in some cases, steps—that you will take in order to make your goals a reality. Instead of daydreaming about a change—rolling around in a bathtub full of cash in retirement or walking around on the beach with more abs than can be counted with the human eye—you focus on the actions that *cause* the change you're after. Process goals are about one thing: taking action. They are the very steps we will take to move closer to our top goals.

Knowing how your process goals will feed into your outcome goals is paramount. This is why a significant part of goal attainment is planning. Of course, any amount of time we spend planning is time that we won't spend actually making progress. But generally, we plan too little and not too much.

As it relates to our goals, we tend to think of the ratio of planning to action as something like 95 percent action and 5 percent planning. **The reality, though, is closer to 80 percent action and 20 percent planning.**

Twenty percent seems like a high number, and if you are anything like I was, this is more planning than you have traditionally engaged in. But there is a reason that more planning has such a large payoff: There are so many levels across which we can act deliberately—all the layers of the Intention Stack.

The rituals that help us accomplish more of our intentions are typically ones that lead us to consider how our short- and long-term intentions are connected with one another. We can become more intentional in each moment, each month, each quarter, and throughout our whole lives. Because we work toward our larger intentions across all these time frames, it's critical that we examine them all, so a goal can actually fit into our busy life.

As a quote (inaccurately) ascribed to Abraham Lincoln puts it, "Give me six hours to chop down a tree and I will spend the first four sharpening the axe."[6]

With our ratios here, one hour of the six ought to cut it.

It's immensely helpful to set a process goal for each outcome goal that you have, especially at the inception of a goal. By using your initial burst of motivation for planning rather than execution, you can lock in your motivation to create lasting, real change.

Let's say you have an outcome goal of developing a consistent daily meditation practice. Starting out, the best process goal might be to observe which of your daily habits are revving up your mind the most and are getting in the way of your daily sit. Then you can move on to process goals that are about actually meditating consistently—such as building a streak of ten consecutive days. (It's worth noting that if you can't muster the motivation to plan how you will achieve a large goal that you set, you in all likelihood won't have the motivation to follow through with the goal after your initial motivation wanes.)

Once you've established a process goal, don't be afraid to revise it as your outcome goal evolves, you discover more efficient ways of taking action, or your goal is no longer an ambition for you because it has turned into a habit. (Practiced consistently, our deliberate intentions can turn into our default intentions, which we practice automatically.) You'll likely need to throw a decent amount of proverbial spaghetti at the wall to see what sticks. Experiment with as many process goals as you can to find the one that contributes the most to your desired outcomes. For example, if your goal is to learn how to play the piano, if you're anything like me, you'll need to cycle through a bunch of processes to find the one that works—and that you'll enjoy following through with. Maybe you'll cycle through goals like practicing with a piano app, improvising to feel out which notes sound best together, or learning your favorite songs until you settle on the goal that works best: to hire a skilled piano teacher who also holds you accountable.

Generally speaking, the process goals you nest inside your outcome goals should be compelling to do and let you make the greatest amount of progress for the least amount of time, attention, and energy. Near the end of this chapter, in the goal inventory exercise, I'll share a few of my current process goals that I'm using to achieve my outcome goals.

Again, these goals are constantly evolving—as they should.

Experience Goals

It is worth noting that in some rare cases, the processes and outcomes for your goals will be the same. This is particularly true when your goal is to *experience* something on a regular basis. Intentions to meditate daily or savor episodes of your favorite show fall into this category. Examples like these are rare, however; they are the "exceptions that prove the rule." Even if you don't have any goals that naturally fit into this category, it could be worth setting one. Not every experience has to contribute to some predefined accomplishment— and in a lot of cases, it can be more enjoyable when they don't.

Rate of Progress

Once you've determined your outcome goal and the process goals through which you'll achieve it, it's worth also keeping tabs on the rate at which you are making progress. All three factors are intertwined: your rate of progress is determined by the intensity of your process goals, which lead you closer to your outcomes.

Tracking your rate of progress across your goals is simple. First, it is worth determining roughly how much time you'll have to devote to your goals each week. For a nice round number, let's say you can spare five hours a week to your goals.

The key in doing this is to always look for ways to get the biggest "bang for your buck" with your goals—while making progress in all the areas you would like to. Certain actions will lead to greater progress for each of your outcome goals. For example, focusing on automating a repetitive work task will likely result in far greater progress than a plan to focus on the same task more intensely every day. Work to discover these "high-leverage" uses of your time as you refine your goals over the timeline of goal attainment with the amount of time you have.

At the start, you're unlikely to accurately estimate how much time (and attention and energy) you have for your goals. That's okay, because it's easy to calibrate over time. Much like a goal itself, the key is to estimate a starting point for the resources you'll have to follow through on it, rather than nail the amount head-on. Pick a number to start with and adjust from there.

This ritual is simple, but it adds needed structure to our goals, while accommodating our constraints.

There are a few things to keep in mind when setting your rate of progress.

BE FLEXIBLE

If you've ever set a strict schedule for yourself only to break it, or you realize your goal requires more time than you currently have, or you get a sudden bout of illness that puts you out of commission for a few days, you know how hard it is to maintain a consistent rate of progress. Our rates of progress fluctuate over time—and the good news is, this is totally natural.

The reality is, we don't have unlimited time, attention, energy, and resources to devote to our goals—daily life can be demanding enough. What each goal asks of you will also evolve over time, and occasionally, the sum of the resources your goals require will exceed your capacity.

Let's assume you're working toward two goals: writing a novel and building up your strength. You have a consistent one-hour lunch break every day to put toward these goals. Even with the same amount of discretionary time, there will be spikes and dips in how much time each of your process goals requires. Maybe you love hitting the gym during your lunch hour on Mondays, Wednesdays, and Fridays. These days, you'll have less time for working on your novel. Or maybe you'll sit down to write and realize you're too wiped out after a morning of back-to-back meetings, and a workout is really what you have capacity for.

This is why it's important to consider resource fluctuations like these in our goal planning—including for resources like attention and energy, which are harder to track. Because we don't account for the fact that our goals compete for the same limited pool of resources, we often end up dropping goals not because we want to but because we feel overwhelmed. Given our limited resources, it's worth becoming more intentional about which goals are truly worth the investment.

If any of this sounds discouraging, remember, it's entirely possible to achieve all the goals you set! Just keep in mind that your capacity to make progress on a lot of goals at the same time is constrained by your available resources. To quote David Allen, the author of *Getting Things Done*, "You can do *anything*, but not *everything*" (emphasis mine).[7]

PICK FAVORITES

If you find you're not making as much progress as you'd like, you may need to "pick favorites," slowing down the rates of progress on certain outcome goals by dialing back how ambitious your process goals are. Calibrate your goals downward during times when resources are more constrained—like during a busy period at work or when your child is sick—and make them more ambitious when you have more resources at your disposal. You can do this during a weekly goal review, which I'll cover at the end of the chapter.

I find that my own resources fluctuate wildly over time—including around the busy seasons in my work and life. When I'm on a book deadline, I need to dial back my other projects, just as I need to put some of my personal goals on pause while I'm on vacation. You'll have similar factors that influence your own resources. Productivity is often a process of understanding—and working around—your constraints.

ACCOUNT FOR DESIRE AND AVERSION

On top of resource fluctuations, the amount of desire we have to achieve our goals—and the amount of aversion we have to doing them—also fluctuates, affecting our rate of progress. Goals are typically most inspiring as we first set them, but over time this desire can taper off into aversion. (Just think about the New Year's resolutions that have faded in your past.)

Remember, there is some amount of aversion in every goal you set—even if the amount is minuscule. (If there weren't, you probably would have achieved the goal already!) For instance, although you really want to pursue a career change to escape your stressful job, you may still have a bit of resistance because of the fear of the unknown.

There are ways of adapting a goal to make it less aversive—which we'll cover in the next chapter—but what you need to know for now is that the more aversive a goal is, the less you'll want to do it, and the more mental resources it'll eat up from other pursuits. So when establishing your rate of progress, **the less you want to do something, the shorter your process goal's duration should be.** This means that process goals that are more aversive should reside farther down the Intention Stack and take place over a shorter amount of time.

For example, let's say you set a goal to write an average of 250 words of your novel every day this year. You really want to write this novel, but the idea of sitting down every single day this year to write is aversive to you. Instead, you might decide to schedule three short, focused writing sessions every week this *month*. Shorter timelines make goals more tangible and let you better see how they fit into your daily and weekly life.

The more aversion you tame ahead of time, the more ambitious your goals can be—while consuming the same amount of resources.

Desire, on the other hand, is trickier to manage. There are a lot of variables that affect what we desire, which we'll dig into in chapter 5. But for now, let's explore how desire fluctuates, making certain goals harder to achieve.

DESIRE CURVES

Something you'll find as you achieve more of your goals—and as you bring greater awareness to the ideas in this book—is that different tactics will work better or worse for you depending on how committed you are to achieving a goal. One big reason for this is that our level of desire and aversion fluctuate according to where we are in our timeline of goal attainment. For example, a lot of goals (if not most of them) are somewhat sepia-toned at the start—in other words, we romanticize them. Fresh out the gate, with a newfound intention to lose ten pounds, our motivation will rarely be higher. Two months in, down seven pounds and trying to stick to our diet plan as we're sitting in front of a delicious funnel cake at a restaurant, the exact opposite may be true.

We all have spikes and dips in motivation like these. This tug-of-war between desire and aversion is a bit curious to watch as our progress unfolds.

At any given time, we can find the attractiveness of a goal by comparing our desire to achieve something with our level of aversion. If we chart these values over the timeline of a goal, it's even possible to sketch out a "desire curve," which is how our overall level of desire fluctuates.

Take, for example, a goal of doing a "polar dip" this winter, where you'll plunge into icy waters to raise money for charity. Your level of desire may be quite high for most of the timeline of the goal—when you're far away from having to do the dip—but you'll probably also experience a colossal spike in aversion the day you have to jump into the water.

Desire Curve: Polar Dip

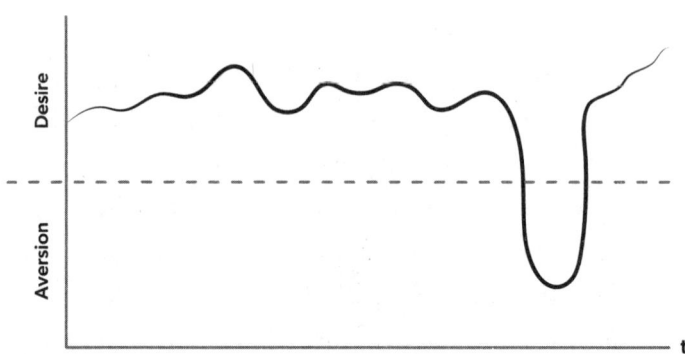

Other goals, like learning a new language, may fluctuate wildly across the entire timeline. If you have a goal to learn Spanish for an upcoming trip, your level of desire may greatly outweigh your level of aversion at the start, when you've decided to go on the trip. A few months later, once you book your flight, your desire level may spike once again. But this desire may also turn into aversion once the novelty of the original goal fades and as other intentions compete for the same pool of time and attention. Your level of aversion may spike again once your language lessons become more tedious and you see the long road ahead of you.

Desire Curve: Learn Spanish

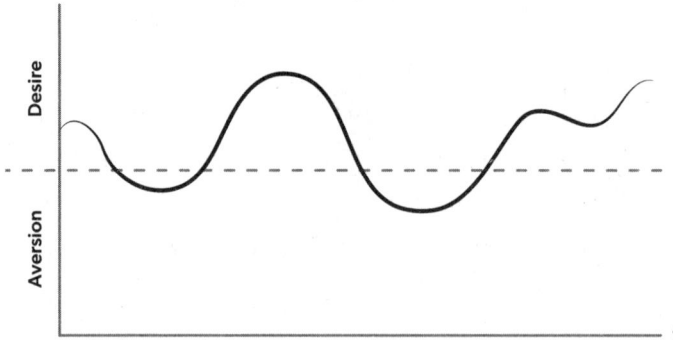

Some goals may have a high or low overall level of desire throughout. If you're planning a wedding, your level of excitement and desire may be quite high all the way up to the big day. You may not need to do much to motivate yourself to get things done as a result. On the flip side, if you're in the middle of decluttering your home, the goal may prove aversive the entire way through, and you may need all the help you can get to tame aversion and maximize desire.

I'd be lying if I said that I estimated my desire timelines for every goal I set, or even for most of them. But explicitly drawing out how you expect your desire to tackle a goal will ebb and flow over time is a remarkably helpful strategy for goals you really want to achieve—including ones for which you believe your initial desire will at some point taper into aversion. For especially challenging goals, reflecting on how your levels of aversion and desire will fluctuate—or have already fluctuated—can prove enormously helpful for overcoming obstacles that will get in your way down the line. (This tactic is included, alongside all the others in the book, in chapter 8.)

As with goals themselves, a desire curve is a simple prediction, and many of the ones you sketch out will differ from the reality you will experience. Just do what you can to anticipate both desire and aversion ahead of time. Doing so may help you to channel your energy in a different way, like spending more time planning a goal at its inception rather than actually making progress at the start.

THE GOAL INVENTORY

We don't often (if ever) step back to take stock of all the goals we're working to accomplish—so let's take a minute to do just that. It's great to see all the goals you're working toward in one place, and it can feel refreshing to get them out of your head and into some external place where you can see and manage them. Conducting an inventory also helps you better identify how you can make greater progress while identifying the goals that are no longer serving you.

To make a goal inventory, write down all the current goals you're working toward. Don't think too hard about them—just get them out of your head and write down all that you can possibly think of. Capture everything: goals large and small, short and long, meaningful and meaningless. When you hit a point where you can't think of any more, keep the list somewhere visible that you can easily access—like as a file on your computer's desktop or a sheet of paper on your desk. This way you can remember to write down anything you missed. The key is to get everything out of your head so you can begin planning your goals logically.

Once you have a preliminary list of goals, go back and make sure each has an outcome, process, and a rate of progress that accounts for the interplay between the two. For example, one of my current intentions is to "build a peaceful mind"—that's my broader outcome goal. Nested under this is my current process goal, to "meditate for twenty minutes every morning, at 8:05, with Ardyn" (my wife). And underneath this, to account for the interplay between the two goals, is my current pace, "fast and steady." On my list, I write out the elements so that they're nested within each other, with the process underneath the outcome, because it's farther down the Intention Stack.

> OUTCOME: **Build a resilient, strong, peaceful mind to support my mental health.**
>
> → PROCESS: Meditate for one hour every workday, and in the morning with Ardyn.
>
> → PACE: Fast and steady

Often, your larger outcome goals will require more than one process. If that's the case, write down all the process goals that serve your outcome and group them together, as well as their different rates of progress. Then group related outcome goals under respective buckets like health, work, or creativity.

Here are my current goals, copied and pasted from the Current Goals note on my computer. Keep in mind that I've refined things to this point over time, dropping a lot of goals along the way. I personally separate my intentions into two different contexts, work and personal.

WORK

OUTCOME: **Write *Intentional* in the most helpful way that I can.**

→ PROCESS: Reflect more than I write—while staying on weekly word target.

→ RATE OF PROGRESS: Fast

→ PROCESS: Deeply understand the scientific research behind human intentionality.

→ RATE OF PROGRESS: Medium

OUTCOME: **Operate a sustainable business.**

→ PROCESS: Continue to keep one year of financial runway; revisit monthly.

→ RATE OF PROGRESS: Steady, on-target

OUTCOME: **Create Overcoming Procrastination course and make it surprisingly delightful.**

→ PROCESS: Solidify course structure and filming details.

→ RATE OF PROGRESS: Medium

PERSONAL

OUTCOME: Build a resilient, strong, peaceful mind.

➡ **PROCESS:** Meditate for one hour every workday and in the morning with Ardyn.

➡ **RATE OF PROGRESS:** Fast and steady

OUTCOME: Maintain current level of body fat.

➡ **PROCESS:** Track daily calories and follow habit points sheet.

➡ **RATE OF PROGRESS:** Medium

OUTCOME: Rebuild cardiovascular system to support long-term fitness.

➡ **PROCESS:** Invest in Couch to 10K program.

➡ **RATE OF PROGRESS:** Fast

As you conduct this inventory, you'll likely find that there are a lot of goals you're working toward, some far stronger than others. This realization brings us to the next natural step in creating good goals: revising them.

EDITING YOUR GOALS

You probably won't set the right process and outcome goals at first— it usually takes a few refinements to home in on what you're truly after. Expect to experiment with different process goals to find the routines that lead you to the most progress for how much time and effort you have to spend. Throughout this process, your rate of progress with each of your goals will fluctuate.

But rest assured, fluctuation is all part of the activity of goal attainment. Embrace it. As your goals evolve, you'll accumulate greater and greater progress—which is why you also need to review those goals frequently.

However, week in and week out, as you make your goals more in line with what you would like to accomplish, you may find that some goals that sounded worthwhile on the surface, in practice feel a bit . . . off. Maybe, despite tweaking your process goals to adjust for your current level of desire and aversion, you just can't keep up momentum. Maybe you're questioning whether an outcome will still be worth the resources required to make it happen.

Just because a goal is a struggle doesn't mean that it isn't worthwhile. Some of your most worthwhile goals *will* prove difficult: writing a book, running a marathon, and getting into the best shape of your life included. But we must always examine *why* we're struggling with a goal. Sometimes we struggle because a goal is hard—a good kind of struggle that is part of doing challenging, meaningful things. Other times, struggle is a sign that a goal is not a good fit for who we are, because the goal represents some ideal, not some tangible improvement we are endeavoring to make to our life or to our days, or because it's not in line with what we truly value.

It can be difficult to tell which goals are worthwhile and which ones need to be revised until we try them on for size. The key is to hold our list of current intentions a bit more loosely—while keeping in mind some of the reasons a goal may be worth dropping. For some goals on our list, a different version of the same overarching goal may be a better fit.

Other times, despite having adjusted our process goals, it still proves difficult to move toward certain goals. This may be a sign we need to reconsider why something is a goal in the first place.

Sepia-Toned Goals

Not every goal that *feels* or *sounds* right will prove worthwhile. I've found that this is especially the case for goals that promise to bring some "idealized state of being"—only once you have achieved them.

Unfortunately, sometimes the idea of a goal is disconnected from the daily reality of what it will take to achieve it. We fall in love with the *idea* of a goal, pushing out of mind how different our day-to-day will need to be for us to make it happen. In fact, research even suggests that positive fantasies about our future can lead us to put *less* effort into our goals because our fantasies provide us with a false and premature sense of accomplishment. We romanticize a goal—falling in love with the idea of a change. In the process, we gloss over the intricacies and challenges of integrating a complex new behavior into our life. As one study nicely summed it up, fantasizing about a positive future "seduces a person to mentally enjoy the desired future in the here and now"—and because we don't reflect on *why* our fantasy is not yet our future, "a necessity to act is not induced."[8]

The goals I've struggled with the most fit into this category and have involved some fantasy I've constructed of how different my life will be once I accomplish them. To illustrate this, there's one goal that immediately comes to mind: to wake up at 5:30 every morning. This is an intention I've set for myself multiple times over the years—I absolutely love the idea of it. And like any good outcome goal, this ideal makes for some strong motivational propellant to dive headfirst into the new ritual. (Some lessons, it seems, we have to learn repeatedly before they stick.)

Every time I try this, I find that I have constructed some beautiful, sepia-toned fantasy of how my days will be different. I imagine waking up—before the sun and the rest of the world—to make a hot cup of coffee, read the newspaper, and get a morning burst of exercise in. I imagine getting to inbox zero before everyone I know even wakes up. (*Wow, this guy is so productive!* they will think.) I picture quietly doing chores around the house while I listen to a podcast, and doing other savory, holy tasks with my morning hours.

Each time, things could not go more differently—maybe even comically so, given that I'm a night owl at heart. In the morning, I need whatever is the mental equivalent of a spatula to pry myself out of bed, because 5:30 a.m. is well before my body wants to get up. At night, I have to go to bed when my friends want to hang out, when I have the most energy and focus, and when more interesting events (sports, concerts, and more) are happening.

As glorious as my outcome-goal daydreams are, waking up that early is simply not a good fit for my biology, interests, or preferred way to live my life. As my mushy morning brain has put it as I've stared at the ceiling at 5:31: *This goal is stupid and it sucks.*

Sometimes, you might achieve your idealized goal and realize it's not truly the way you want to live, that your ideal does not match your reality. I still remember the first time I finally managed to become an early riser. I had built the perfect morning routine, the one that sepia-toned productivity fantasies are made of. I woke up at 5:30 and did all the things I mentioned: drank a cup of coffee, read the paper, and meditated. I worked out, caught up on email, and was otherwise productive. Unfortunately, I still hated the ritual—it did not live up to the fantasy whatsoever. Not even close. Even after successfully integrating it into my life, I felt as though I was sleepwalking through my morning routine and heading to bed when it wasn't yet time to wind down. My days were different—but not in the way I expected or predicted. And definitely not in the way I really wanted.

Author Annie Dillard once wrote that "how we spend our days is, of course, how we spend our lives."[9] Following this thread, for our life to be different, our *days* need to be different. This is why to make progress on our goals, we must focus on the outcome *and* the process—balancing our fantasies with realistic planning. We must consider the future we want to create *and* the process that will get us there.

Tucked away inside every fantasy about a better life is a whole lot of work—and typically a hidden set of compromises. Eventually, ideals collide with reality, and we discover how much of a challenge it is to work a goal into our everyday life—or just how many mental, physical, and emotional resources a goal eats up.

In reflecting on and reviewing your goals, remember that some will lead you to a real difference and others may be more sepia-toned fantasies. It's up to you to decide which ones you want.

Values Misalignments

Sometimes, we may repeatedly struggle to attain a goal, struggling because it isn't aligned with what we value. A number of these types of goals may need to be dropped, and we'll talk about that in a minute. However, more often than not, goals that are misaligned with our values benefit more from an edit or reframe. There is often a different yet similar goal that gets us to the same outcome we're aiming at, but that better accommodates our values, motivations, and constraints.

It's easiest to illustrate this with an example.

Let's take the standard goal I've been mentioning throughout this chapter: losing a bit of body fat. (This is a good general example, especially because one study conducted by Ipsos found that in 2021, 45 percent of people *globally* were trying to lose weight.[10])

To achieve this end, an obvious starting goal might be to lose ten pounds over the next six months in order to have a six-pack by beach season.

This is a nicely structured outcome goal—but it could be stronger.

Notice that this goal is most connected with the value of "face"— how we come across to others—because it is framed in a way that mentions how we want to appear to other people. But maybe you value health, self-direction, or conformity more than you care about how you're perceived. If that's the case, here's how you might tweak the goal.

For a health value goal, you could set a goal to eat as cleanly as possible for one month, while also noting all the mental and physical improvements you feel along the way. If you value self-direction, maybe you want to experiment with five different ways of eating cleanly over the next two months to find the best one for you. If you value conformity more than anything else, finding an accountability partner who you don't want to let down may be the most effective strategy.

The interesting thing about this example is how the actions you can take to achieve all three of these specific goals might be *exactly the same*. For example, you could settle on eating a whole-food, plant-based diet for five days every week—something that leads you to accomplish all the above ambitions. The difference is in how you frame each goal for yourself.

Goals that fit with who you truly are will lead you to far greater progress while still being relatively effortless. Reframing your goals through a values-based edit can make them downright more enjoyable.

I'll be sprinkling some additional values ideas throughout the book ahead of diving into values tactics in chapter 6. But in the current context of goal editing, know that a large reason a goal may need revising is that you simply don't care about it enough. As a result, it doesn't motivate you. Yet if there's still something about the goal that you find compelling—and the goal doesn't feel like an overidealized sepia-toned fantasy—it may just be that you haven't found the right value frame for your goal yet.

Remember that goals become easier when they fit with who you are. They won't feel like an obligation—they'll feel like an opportunity to act in accordance with your personal nature. The goals you feel deeply compelled to achieve—that you've been struggling to achieve for some time—may greatly benefit from a reframe so that they contribute to what you value most. In the process of doing this, you can better zero in to what you're truly after.

Remember that your goals exist to serve *you*—not the other way around.

OBLITERATING OBSTACLES

Another tactic to consider as you edit your goals—a tactic that has been reported on in hundreds of research articles—is called mental contrasting.

Across the timeline of each of your goals, obstacles will arise. You already know this. After all, this is one factor that makes our goals more of a prediction than our destined reality. But, despite how many obstacles have arisen in your past, how often have you stepped back to anticipate the obstacles that will get in the way of your goals in the *future*? My answer, before I read the research, was: not often.

Mental contrasting is dead simple yet remarkably helpful. To practice it, pick a goal from your list, preferably one that'll require a longer period of time, during which you're likely to encounter plenty of obstacles. Then, imagine successfully completing the goal in the future—celebrating hitting a point of financial freedom, stepping onto your scale in the morning and seeing your goal weight before your very eyes, or holding a beautiful hardcover book in your hands that has your name printed on the front.

As we covered earlier, daydreaming about successfully finishing a goal isn't that helpful and can detract from the motivation you have. But in mental contrasting, you don't stop at visualization. After thinking about attaining a goal, you then think about and imagine all the obstacles that will get in your way between now and your point of goal attainment.

With financial freedom, did you have to prioritize saving money after the arrival of your first kid, when doing so was toughest? With hitting your goal weight, did you have to give up sugar—or maybe eat more of it if your goal was to gain weight? With writing a book, did you have to stop watching TV in the evening to spend that time writing instead?

What will get in your way?

Start by identifying the main hurdle you will need to overcome with a goal. Then, to make the tactic even more helpful and work it into the system you have developed, consider defining a new process goal to home in on the obstacle. By doing so, you direct your focus at obliterating the largest obstacle that is getting between you and your goal. When you notice your rate of progress dip, try doing the edit again to accelerate your progress and eliminate new obstacles that will inevitably arise.

While the technique of mental contrasting is simple, it holds immense power. It helps us step into the shoes of our future selves to imagine a future that we will create for ourselves and others.

Crucially, mentally contrasting our future with our path to making it happen also helps us consider all levels of the Intention Stack—the entire timeline between where we are today and where we wish to be tomorrow.

THE GOAL REVIEW

Let me share one of my favorite rituals for revising your goals. The various puzzle pieces I've mentioned in this chapter—outcome and process goals, rates of progress, sepia-toned fantasies, and misaligned values—will all fall into place in this exercise. I call it the goal review.

There are three relatively simple steps:

1. **Review** your current goals.

2. **Update** your goals.

3. **Plan** how you'll follow through on your process goals before your next review.

Step one, **review**, is self-explanatory. Start by reviewing your goal inventory—your list of outcomes, processes, and rates of progress—to bring all your goals to the forefront of your mind. This primes the pump for the next two steps. At this point, certain intentions may stick out to you more than others. Maybe you'll see intentions you haven't made progress on in a while; maybe some of your goals need editing; perhaps you'll discover that some of your rates of progress are off, or you want to make space for new goals.

That's where step two, **update**, comes in. Look through your current goals and make changes where they're needed. Some of your process goals will need a minor or major edit—like to lower them in the Intention Stack so they take place over a shorter amount of time and become less aversive and more tangible. Sometimes your outcomes will need an edit to account for where your processes are taking you—or so you can change course for where you'd like to go or to better accommodate what you value. You might occasionally find that some goals you originally thought would be a good fit for your life are sepia-toned goals in disguise, or completely misaligned with your values in a way that's a bit funny in hindsight. If this is the case, consider editing them so they serve you better. Again: Your goals are there to serve *you*—not the other way around.

Your rates of progress may also need updating. To define my pace of progress for each goal, I'll typically just jot down the speed at which I'm currently making progress (e.g., slow, medium, fast). For maintenance goals—goals I have already achieved and now want to keep going with, like continuing with my meditation practice—I'll assess how steadily I'm conserving the progress I've made. Occasionally, I won't yet have enough data to determine my pace of progress and will leave the field temporarily empty. These are the labels that work for me—use them if you'd like, or use your own, perhaps by specifying the frequency at which a specific process goal takes place. Whatever progress label you use, write down how quickly (or not) you're making progress with your intentions. If you find that your rate of progress is low for a goal, but you'd like it to be higher, that can be a good cue for you to try out a different process goal or two, or to up the intensity of the one you already have.

The final step is to **plan**. If you do this ritual once a week—a good cadence for making steady and consistent progress—consider what needs to be done to further your goals in the week ahead. (I like conducting the ritual on Sunday, so I can review my list before the week begins.) Not every goal will require effort every week—for example, you may have some goals related to saving money that are more relevant at the start of each month. For goals that benefit from consistent effort, however, plan exactly how you'll act on them, like by doing the following:

- Scheduling blocks of time devoted to chipping away at your goal (e.g., two hours after work on Tuesday and three hours Saturday morning).

- Using mental contrasting to identify obstacles that will get in the way of your goals in the week ahead (e.g., a time- and attention-consuming upcoming presentation you will have to prepare for).

- Setting up reminders, calendar events, or other notifications to remind yourself to take action.

- Asking a friend or loved one to join you in a goal (e.g., to join you for a workout at the gym, for a writing session, or a morning meditation ritual).

- Considering how much time, attention, and energy you'll have to act on your goals, to adjust your ambitions accordingly, and account for your current resources.

Creating an intention review ritual may sound easy—the steps for doing one will feel natural, if not obvious in hindsight. But in this simplicity lies immense power: You'll not only consider your goals on a regular cadence but you'll also make consistent, steady progress, while thinking through exactly how you will need to act toward your current intentions.

For acting more deliberately and accomplishing more—and, over the longer arc of time, editing and trying out more goals—I think you'll find that this ritual, along with the ideas in this chapter, are in a league all their own.

DROPPING GOALS

Something that doesn't get nearly enough airtime in productivity books is how we should be abandoning some of our goals. Doing this is more of an opportunity than it is an admission of defeat: Over time, the more goals we abandon, the more goals we get the opportunity to try on for size.

Think of it this way: If you inherit $50 million from a rich uncle you never knew existed, one option is to set a goal to blow every last cent of it on a ridiculous new yacht. But at some point, you may come to your senses and consider that these resources could also be spent elsewhere—and in a way that might bring you and others more joy, happiness, and fulfillment.

This is especially important when a goal is incompatible with what you value, and you've tried and failed to frame it within another value. At that point, it can be wise to drop the goal entirely. For example, say you value achievement and power far more than you value universalism. If one of your goals is to live off the grid in order to reduce your carbon footprint, that goal may be so misaligned with your values that it doesn't motivate you at all. In a case like this, the goal may be worth dropping—possibly in service of a completely different goal that accomplishes a similar result, such as forming a task force within your company to become a global leader in clean energy.

As with financial investments, there is always an opportunity cost behind every goal we pursue: options we are saying no to by saying yes to something else and investing those resources elsewhere. Remember, our time, energy, and attention are limited. Sometimes we have to drop a goal to make sure we have enough of these to make another goal happen.

Right now, you may not know which of your current goals are worth dropping entirely. That's normal—there are goals I'm in the *middle of* that I'm still not entirely sure about! (Here's looking at you, *No eating after dinner.*) It's worth reiterating that this uncertainty is all part of the process—in other words, and I say this in the politest way possible, get used to it!

You may be surprised by what fits best. Just as not all tasks in our work are created equal, not every goal is created equal. Keep in mind, as you review your goals, that some may be worth dropping—if only so you can try on others for size.

BY NOW, we've covered a decent amount of ground for determining what characteristics goals should and shouldn't have. By default, some of the goals we set are more of a prediction than they are a tangible change we will make to our life (and to our days). On top of this, some of our goals are more like idealized fantasies, while others aren't aligned with what we value.

By capturing and expanding on our intentions—by setting both process- and outcome-based goals and by writing down our current rates of progress—we zero in on what we are aiming to accomplish, determine how we will make progress, and understand how quickly we will do so. We also have a stronger starting place from which to make adjustments over time. Whether we adjust the outcomes we're predicting, the processes we're actioning, or our rate of progress, by making course corrections we step closer toward our goals with time.

If you take off in an airplane aimed exactly where you expect to go, there will be things that may steer you off course: the wind, changes in air pressure, and unexpected turbulence included. The same is true for goals. We always take off pointed directly at our initial ambition, but the complexity of life invariably steers us off course. Goal attainment can be messy. Fortunately, by consistently reviewing and revising our goals, we continue to move toward them—even when it feels as though we're flying sideways.

4

Ugly Goals

"If you take too long in deciding what to do
with your life, you'll find you've done it."
—*Anonymous*

By now in the book, you've established your outcome goals and have set process goals to move toward them. You may have also started to keep track of your progress and even account for fluctuations in your time, attention, and energy. Maybe you've also done a values edit or two. However, the process goals you set can begin to break down—not for lack of desire to accomplish them but because the goal that was once motivating has become more aversive with time.

While we must set strong intentions to follow through on our goals, intentions, as we've learned, get us only halfway there. To twist an old phrase, intentions can lead us to water, but they can't make us drink. There is often a gap between the intentions we set and what we end up doing. Sometimes this gap is a small one we can step over. Other times it looks more like a chasm.

The chapters to come will help you bridge these intention gaps so you can do more of what you set out to do. In the process, we'll move up the Intention Stack, carving out space to make our goals more of a priority in our daily life.

There are a bunch of reasons intention gaps exist. Sometimes they're there because we haven't spent enough time thinking through and structuring our goals. That's the subject of most of this book, especially chapter 7. Other times, we haven't cultivated enough desire to propel us forward to the point of goal attainment—the subject of the next chapter. Then there are the times when, like a tin can, aversion leads us to kick our intentions down the street for another day—for our future selves to do—a phenomenon known as procrastination. That's the subject of this chapter.

IMPULSIVE PROCRASTINATION

Every one of our goals—along with the intentions they give rise to—contains some combination of aversion and desire. These are opposing forces: While desire attracts us toward a goal, aversion repels us away.

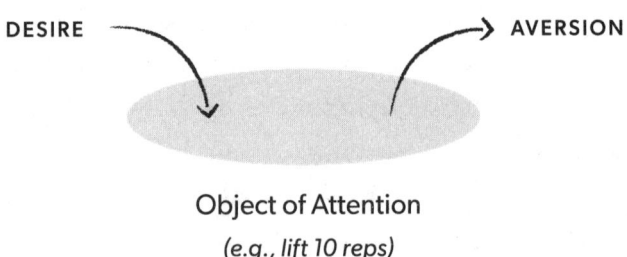

DESIRE   AVERSION

Object of Attention
(e.g., lift 10 reps)

Research shows that this opposition even has neurological roots, with implications within the depths of our brain. In deciding whether to do something, we will always consider the costs and benefits of taking action. We weigh the *rewards* of completing a task against the *negative emotions* we will experience while doing so. As this happens, two separate pathways in our brain compete with each other for dominance. One is related to logic, the other to emotion. Thinking about and desiring the valuable outcomes of finishing something, our brain's hippocampus (involved in memory and imagining future rewards) and caudate nucleus (also involved in reward processing as well as motivation) talk to each other more and we consider how a task might be valuable and rewarding. At the same time, connections between our amygdala (which flags emotional salience) and insula (which processes aversion) increase when we find a task *un*appealing—the strength of this connection generates the negative emotions that lead us to both aversion and procrastination.[1] (Aversion and procrastination are two sides of the same coin.)

Through this lens, procrastination can be viewed as a battle between logic and emotion. Either we take action or, as renowned procrastination researcher and emeritus psychology professor at Carleton University in Ottawa Tim Pychyl likes to put it, we "give in to feeling good."[2]

The fact that this response is hardwired in us indicates something remarkable: Procrastination is a *built-in impulse*, a feature of our brain that is really a response to the way we feel about certain tasks. As Tim put it to me, "Procrastination isn't a time-management problem—it's an emotion-regulation problem."

Some of us tend to irrationally delay our behavior more than others. This will especially be the case if you're impulsive—the character trait most highly correlated with increased procrastination. Impulsiveness is a trait I personally have in spades. If there's a bag of chips in the house, I'll eat it—and sometimes won't be able to think about anything else unless I do. If I don't have a distractions blocker (which prevents me from visiting news and social media websites) enabled when I write, I'll invariably drift to checking emails. Fortunately, we can accommodate our (nonclinical) impulsiveness through the ideas we'll talk about in this chapter.

On the opposite end of the spectrum, the more conscientious you are and the more you value achievement, the *less* likely you are to procrastinate.

We all have a different default propensity to procrastinate. Yet the phenomenon is widespread: Students report spending about a third of their day procrastinating, while 15 to 20 percent of adults procrastinate chronically.[3] Given the very human tendency to procrastinate, it should come as no surprise that the research shows pretty much every one of us procrastinates on a regular basis.

And it's not a new phenomenon—procrastination was widespread throughout history. One of the earliest known records of procrastination comes from Hesiod, an ancient Greek poet who wrote around 700 BC: "And do not put things off till the next day or the day after. For a man who is an idle worker will not fill his granary by putting things off. Attention to your work will make the yield increase."[4] Another sound piece of advice from elsewhere in his book: "When you are building a house, do not leave it rough-hewn, or a cawing crow may settle on it and croak." (Take note, home builders.)

To sum it up, procrastination is irrational, emotional, hardwired, and above all else, human.

It's also triggered by something specific: the characteristics of aversion.

THE CHARACTERISTICS OF AVERSION

Assuming you made a goal inventory in the last chapter, chances are good that at least one of the goals on your list is highly aversive.

There's a very easy way to tell whether a goal has little aversion and is a high priority for you: You've achieved it already! Or, if you're in the middle of getting it done, you have to put little thought and effort into making progress. Sepia-toned and values-misaligned goals aside, there are reasons you haven't yet achieved the things on your list. Sometimes the reason is, as we discussed in the previous chapter, a lack of resources or desire. Other times, the reason may be aversion.

There are a bunch of characteristics that make a goal aversive and make us more likely to put it off. As you read the following list, try doing so slowly, to fully consider each attribute for a second or two. Aversion is curious: Even *reading* the list may make you feel some combination of rebellion and disgust. The six characteristics of aversion[*] occur when a task is

- **boring,**

- **unpleasant,**

- **frustrating,**

- **far off in the future,**

- **unstructured, and**

- **meaningless.**[5]

On top of these characteristics, there are also conditions about the *situation* surrounding a task that make it aversive. If we have **resentment** about having to do something, we become significantly less likely to follow through—we rebel against doing the task to simulate

---

[*] For those readers of my previous book, *The Productivity Project*, in which I briefly discuss the procrastination triggers, you'll notice that these triggers are revised slightly from the ones in that book. This is to reflect more recent research while also considering which triggers affect progress on our goals and intentions—with a focus beyond that of our daily productivity.

regaining control, when we're usually just delaying the inevitable. In fact, if we have a **lack of control** with how or whether we'll complete a task, we become more likely to put it off. Generally, the shorter the **timeline**, the more intense our aversion becomes as well.[6, 7]

For a second, bring to mind a task that you repeatedly put off—like filing your taxes, completing some DIY project in the basement, or studying for a certification or exam. This task likely has several of the aversion characteristics. In the case of filing your taxes, the task sets off pretty much every trigger (though your mileage may vary—the aversion characteristics are highly subjective). Generally speaking, you likely find doing your taxes *boring*—few of us find the process exciting. It's also *unpleasant* and, occasionally, *frustrating* to dig through old paperwork to unearth receipts, invoices, and old returns. Most of us don't find much *meaning* in the activity, either. That said, the activity is typically pretty *structured*—such as when we file an online return that guides us through the steps—and this cuts the aversion somewhat. Because the task sets off many of the triggers for most of us, though, we put the activity off—at least until we can feel the tax-filing deadline approaching, when the activity isn't *far off in the future*.

Aversion sucks. But here's some good news. Research shows that **the more we activate the logical centers in our brain as we pursue our goals, the less aversive we find them, which makes us less likely to procrastinate on them.** By logically planning our path to goal attainment, we give logic a needed push—and often the power and oxygen it needs to win the war that plays out between logic and our emotional impulses.

Thankfully, we have already done this in several ways:

- When we weed out or heavily edit goals that are misaligned with our values or those goals that are sepia-toned, the edited goals become more meaningful and connected with who we are. This makes them far less aversive.

- By thoughtfully defining and updating our goal outcomes, we consider the results of our actions, which lets us process how rewarding our goals are.

- By thinking through our process goals, and the rates of progress that these actions cause, we consider exactly how we'll follow through with our goals. In the process, they become more structured and less aversive.

- When we move our process goals a bit farther down the Intention Stack so that they take place over a shorter period of time, they become more tangible. This moves them closer in time and makes them more structured, which helps with those procrastination triggers.

- By reviewing our goals weekly—or at whatever cadence works best for our preferences and workflows—we make a routine out of logically thinking about and revising our goals.

According to one research summary published in the *Educational Research Review*, methods like these work because they "focus on changing the behavioral pattern of procrastination by using cognitive-behavioral interventions," leading to a "substantial reduction [in] procrastination."[8] A different research summary found the same, that "goal setting [reduces] procrastination."[9] Even when we set goals by using methods that are less than ideal (like with SMART goals), we can lower aversion and procrastinate less.

But as you might guess, our work with aversion is not yet done. We know that over time aversion tends to fluctuate, just like our available resources. It usually increases once our initial period of motivation wanes. For example, you may be uber-motivated to collect paperwork for tax season when you remember that your moving expenses were tax-deductible. But once this burst of motivation fades, tedium sets in and forces of aversion may overpower whatever motivation you have remaining.

This is why it's worth structuring your ugliest goals in a way that minimizes aversion—and tames the triggers of both aversion and procrastination. A bit of forethought can save you a *lot* of wasted time and resources later on, as well as lower how much guilt and anxiety—common emotions we experience while irrationally putting something off in the process of goal attainment.

Let's tame our aversion through tackling each attribute of aversion in turn, beginning with goals that are mind-numbingly boring.

REVERSING BOREDOM

If you were to pore over the prevailing research on goal setting, attainment, and intentionality, one of the first things you'd think is, *Holy smokes, is there ever a lot of it.* There are countless theories about how we should be setting goals—often with a wealth of conflicting evidence concerning which techniques are actually most useful in practice.

Many ideas that sound good on the surface—or ones that are based on a catchy acronym where each letter of a word stands for a step of a process—are often not as wise (or smart) as they first appear. Human behavior is complex and difficult to bottle up into an abbreviation. Luckily for us, though, research does point to a few techniques that make us more likely to achieve our goals—including the strategies we have discussed so far and, most important for our purposes here, the strategy to make goals more **challenging**.[10] In making your goals more challenging you make them more interesting, and you become more likely to achieve them.

The idea of making your goals more challenging may in *itself* be aversive—at least at first blush. Doesn't upping the challenge level of a goal consume more of our precious resources—time, attention, and energy included? But in practice, the reverse proves true: When a goal or task is boring, what is so off-putting about it is precisely that it is not challenging enough. (Besides, procrastination *also* eats up a large amount of our resources—while leaving us feeling guilty when we reflect back at how we've spent our time.)

To illustrate the power of adding a dash of challenge to a goal, imagine that, after a big holiday feast, your family has retired to the living room and left you to wash the dishes by yourself. (They cooked, and you agreed to clean up their mess.) Walking into the kitchen, with the tryptophan coursing through your veins lulling you into a bout of sleepiness, you see towers of dishes in front of you. Most people would see plates and pots and pans; all you can see is the tedium of washing them all. Your shoulders droop as you consider the task ahead. For a fleeting moment, you even contemplate grabbing the baseball bat out of the garage: It'd be a lot easier to just smash everything and start over, right? How much could new dishes cost anyway . . . ?

One way to tackle this is to submit to its boring nature and go through the dull motions of the task. But this may make the task only more aversive. A second, more productive option is to make the task more challenging—preferably in a way you enjoy. For example: Could you make a game out of doing the dishes and have your family bet on how long the dishes will take you? Can you set some artificial deadline for yourself, like to have them all done in twenty minutes and compare your speed with a countdown timer you set right when you start? Could you do the dishes more *slowly*, to enjoy the cleaning by reflecting on the incredible memories of meals you've shared with family on elegant plates that have been in the family for eighty years?

Can you reward yourself with one dollar of frivolous spending for every minute you spend washing those dishes?

For a task like this, stepping back for just a moment to find a way to make it more challenging actually makes back time—especially if you'd procrastinate otherwise.

Doing dishes is probably not on your list of goals or intentions. (Unless it's on your to-do list, which is really just a place where we store the intentions that live near the bottom of the Intention Stack.) But it serves as a nice illustration of how making a task more challenging can truly eliminate boredom.

A few more examples:

- If you're learning a new language, consider signing yourself up for a language proficiency test that you'll be able to ace—but only if you follow through with your goal to learn the language at a certain pace.

- If you find your ongoing goal to keep your home clean and organized tedious, consider a more challenging goal, like running a zero-waste home.

- If you put off regular medical checkups because they're tedious, consider getting more involved with your health by tracking health metrics related to your sleep, diet, and level of physical activity.

But increasing the challenge of a goal doesn't just cancel out boredom. According to one review, it also "can increase the self-satisfaction that arises from completing the difficult rather than the easy."[11]

This is true of goals in general. Simply put, challenging goals are more motivating and lead to a greater amount of action. As usual, it's all about balance: Goals we see as "improbable"—like more challenging goals, sometimes called "stretch goals"—are often really just sepia-toned goals in disguise. Goals like these are not helpful and can even be discouraging. However, research has found that "increased goal difficulty leads to increased goal success," while by comparison, "easy and moderate goals [are] effective but only [have] a small effect compared [with] difficult goals."[12]

For combating boredom, and even increasing your overall satisfaction with how you spend your time, consider upping how challenging your goals are. You'll save time, accomplish more, and procrastinate less as a result.

UPPING ENJOYMENT

A simple truth about productivity—and procrastination—is that **we often put off work, goals, and projects because they're not enjoyable enough**. This doesn't have to be the case. Making work more fun isn't just a matter of putting on rose-colored glasses and seeing the good in all the ugly stuff we have to do. There are real, tangible changes we can make to our goals and projects to make them more enjoyable.

Fortunately, just as there are characteristics of aversion, there are attributes that lead to greater *enjoyment*. These include whether doing something feels:

- connected with our self-identity,

- like something that fills us with passion,

- like it serves others, or

- like it's pleasurable or fun.

The more unpleasant a task is, the more difficult it will be to get started. For making your most aversive tasks more enjoyable, fun, pleasurable, and meaningful, these strategies should help.

Aversion Journaling

Given that our self-identity is constructed around our values—and that what we value leads us to feel passionate about what we're doing—editing your goals so that they're more in line with your true motivational character will make them significantly more fun.

If you find that values editing is not getting you anywhere, however, try journaling.

Perhaps, like me, the thought of journaling puts you off. I was resistant to the practice at first—and honestly, I still kind of am. Writing down a reflection of my day just never stuck for me, as much as I tried to work the habit into my daily routine, and as appealing as the habit feels on the surface. (Your mileage will vary, of course.)

But then I tried journaling in a different way: *between tasks*. Whenever I find that my resistance level is high prior to doing something—especially because that something feels meaningless—I grab the pen and notepad I keep on my desk and write down what I'm about to do, and why exactly it feels so aversive. This small habit allows me to tap into my self-reflective capacity when I need it the most—and saves me time because I'm able to get started more quickly. I can face aversion head-on. In the moment, I never put off this kind of journaling. After all, it feels like an escape from the very task I'm finding aversive.

Journaling about aversion is always less ugly than *actually doing* what you're finding so aversive. In the moment, I give myself a choice: work on what I'm finding aversive or grab a pen and paper to write about why I'm putting it off. I'll invariably grab the pen and paper, because that's less aversive than the task. In doing so, however, I can confront my aversion to deconstruct it and understand it more. This helps me find more exciting ways of approaching what I'm putting off.

I also find that the habit makes me more aware. A big part of doing knowledge work is performing tasks that you don't want to do. Anyone can do simple tasks. But work that's cognitively complex, that requires deep thinking and mental heavy lifting, is aversive by its very nature. It is also sometimes difficult to connect with the meaning behind it. This small habit, of reflecting on this momentary aversion, helps you dissect it in the moment, become more aware of why you're having an aversive reaction to the task, and reflect on how you can make the task more pleasant for yourself.

Make It About Others

When performing values edits to our goals, we can also incrementally improve them so that they're more others-focused rather than self-focused—especially to accommodate our strongest personal values that involve other people, like universalism and benevolence. For example, a goal like "exercise daily to stay fit and healthy" might turn into one to "exercise daily to set a positive example for my students." Or a goal to "read ten pages every day" could turn into one to "read ten pages daily to become a more effective mentor."

When we live in a culture that is highly individualistic, we often gravitate to individual goals by default. Involving others in the goals you're aiming for can make them significantly more inspiring—especially if you're the kind of person who tends to focus on helping others or feels guilty about helping yourself. (You shouldn't.)

Task Pairing

Task pairing is another strategy that is especially helpful for mindless work that doesn't consume your full attention. The idea is to *deliberately multitask* by pairing a less enjoyable task with a more enjoyable one.

For example, if you frequently put off your morning workout, consider allowing yourself to listen to your favorite podcast only at the gym. If you procrastinate by checking social media, use time on social media as a reward for following through with your most aversive task of the day—for every two minutes you spend on the task, you get one minute to spend scrolling through your accounts on neural autopilot mode. Or if you have some dull data entry project to do, consider pairing it with listening to the salacious romance audiobook you've been wanting to listen to—but maybe double-check your work afterward!

When work is mindless and doesn't consume your full attention, use what attention you have to spare to do something enjoyable at the same time. In my book *Hyperfocus,* I write about how multitasking does not work with tasks that require deep concentration—but it can with simpler, habitual tasks that don't require our full attention. Especially if you're procrastinating on the task, what you lose in speed you may more than make up for in how much more time you spend making progress.

Give Yourself a Choice

You can also use a similar strategy to the one I use while journaling: Give yourself a choice between two aversive tasks. I'm not a fan of journaling but also know that aversion journaling helps me save time and accomplish more—so I give myself the choice between either journaling or making progress. A similar strategy can be used for any two aversive tasks. If you're putting off cleaning the basement closet, give yourself a choice between cleaning it or the garage. If you're putting off writing a sensitive email, give yourself a choice between the email and writing a report. In the moment, you'll feel like you have a choice. But really, you're just making a game out of trapping yourself to work on something aversive. If you value self-direction highly, this tactic may be especially helpful.

Gamify It

Making a game out of a task or goal is generally a great way to increase joy and minimize aversion. Writing an essay is boring, but how many words could you crank out in an hour if you focused all your time, attention, and energy on it? Each one-hour sprint, try for a new personal best. Unpacking those moving boxes is an intimidating task, but how many could you finish in twenty minutes? If you can't stand running, download an app that awards you points and gamifies the progress you make—or buy a device like an Apple Watch or Fitbit that does the same. Better yet, download an app like ZRX (Zombies, Run!), where you can simulate being chased by zombies who you have to outrun—or a Couch to 10K app so you can work toward a fun yet challenging goal. The options are endless.

LOWERING FRUSTRATION

Let's tackle another characteristic of aversion that leads us to procrastinate on our goals: frustration. When we feel frustrated as we make progress, this can mean we are working on the wrong type of goal.

Most goals can be characterized as either a **learning goal** or a **performance goal**. Learning goals enable us to develop our knowledge about something, build our skill set, or otherwise expand our competencies. With performance goals, we aim to do a good job relative to other people—or relative to the expectations we have of ourselves. For example, a performance goal to "lose ten pounds" might turn into a learning goal to "educate myself on nutrition principles to live a naturally healthy life that also leads to weight loss." Or a performance goal to "finish running a marathon in under four hours" might turn into one to "learn about advanced running and nutritional techniques to minimize running time during upcoming marathon." The actions we take across both versions of the goal may be the same—but the frame for the goal is different, and it significantly lowers how much frustration we will feel.

We typically have a predisposition toward one type of goal over the other. Research shows that those of us with a learning goal orientation typically approach tasks with an eye toward improving how we do things, while those of us with a performance orientation prefer to do well in order to be viewed positively by others (or to avoid negative judgments). Learning goals are also typically more process-focused in nature, while performance goals are outcome-focused.

Like outcome and process goals, performance and learning orientations both have a place—especially as far as our sense of frustration is concerned. When you must achieve a specific outcome or hit a certain metric, performance goals can be extraordinarily helpful. But when your level of frustration is high, you care about long-term development and adaptability, or you just wish to relate to your goals in a more positive fashion, try framing your goals as learning goals instead.

Learning goals typically involve adopting a "growth mindset"—an idea from renowned Stanford psychologist, professor, and researcher Carol Dweck. With a growth mindset, we believe we can change and improve, which leads us to view challenges as opportunities for growth rather than threats to how well we're performing. We're not so discouraged by feelings of frustration—it's all a part of the process of discovering more about something new.

In one research article, Dweck reports that students who adopt a learning goal become more persistent, enjoy tasks more, and are less frustrated as they encounter challenges.[13] Conversely, a separate study found that those who adopt performance goals often experience higher levels of anxiety and fear failure more, while relying more on external metrics of success—which can lead to frustration when they don't live up to them.[14]

If you find that one of your goals sets off frustration, consider turning it into a learning goal. For example, a goal to save a specific amount of money for the year could turn into one to develop and perfect a stress-free budgeting system for you and your family. If you're frustrated because you're falling behind on your goal to read fifteen personal development books this year, a less frustrating alternative might be to read books from a variety of voices, to discover new ideas and perspectives while you reflect on what each book teaches you.

As always, the actions you take to make progress on both a learning and a performance goal may be exactly the same. The difference is how you relate to your goals, deal with setbacks, and think about progress.

ADJUSTING FOR TIME DISTANCE

On top of certain goals being boring, unpleasant, and frustrating, other goals foster procrastination and resistance because they're so far into the future. The further away a goal is, the less we feel its aversive effects.

On the surface, this sounds like a good thing. Unfortunately, this same time-discounting effect works the other way, too: While feeling less aversion, we also feel significantly less *desire* to make progress on goals that are further out. They're problems that can wait until another day. A study by Shunmin Zhang and Tingyong Feng at Southwest University, which aimed to model how time distance affects procrastination, describes it this way: The further away a reward or loss, "the less impact it has upon decisions."[15]

This is why we feel aversion more when we have to do something *right this moment* compared with some time down the line. Moving to a new city will feel way more daunting one week before the big move compared with a full year out. Similarly, planning a wedding will feel more stressful one week beforehand than it will a full year away. This is common sense, but it underscores a point: With our goals, time distance matters. The further in the future a goal is, the more warped— and faded—it appears from our current vantage point.

But as goals fade, so, too, does our motivation to achieve them, which makes us more likely to procrastinate on making progress. Once we arrive at our designated time to begin working toward a goal, we find that, typically, we have about as much motivation as we did before. Which is to say, not much at all.

Studies show we typically *expect* to have more motivation in the future than we do in the present. In reality, our motivation to get started on a particular goal is relatively consistent over time. As you might expect, given how intertwined aversion and procrastination are, this applies to our delaying tasks, too. Research has found that "procrastinators usually do not stop procrastinating when the future becomes the present."[16]

The aversion we feel when actually taking action is the same: Making a $500 payment on your debt will feel about as aversive six months from now as it does today—though making the payment in six months *sounds* like a piece of cake by comparison with if you're making the decision right now. Think for a second about all the stories you may tell yourself about a goal in the same spirit as this one. *So much can change in six months! I'll probably be making more money! Maybe there'll be hyperinflation!* Alas, your level of aversion and motivation will likely prove consistent over time, because it usually does.

If you find that you're putting off one or two of the goals on your list because they're far away in the future, the solution is the one you might expect: Make long-term goals more relevant and salient to you in the present. There are countless strategies you can deploy to do this. My favorite of the bunch: defining a target pace for the goal.

Define a Target Pace

Whenever I write a book, I have a very specific strategy for both tracking my progress and bringing goals closer to me in time: I track my progress relative to my "target pace."

Here are the steps I take to do this, which work well for any cumulative, long-term goal that requires making consistent progress, and where that progress can be measured—for example, in words written, pounds lost, minutes meditated, or money saved.

1. **Pick a realistic completion date.** This is an essential step—choose a date by which you'll want to have finished your goal. Make this date meaningful. If you're writing a book, have it be the date you promised the manuscript to your editor. If you're writing a project proposal, have the date be a date you promised your CEO the finished report. If you're tracking the miles you run for training for a marathon, have the target date be the date of a marathon you will shortly sign up for.

2. **Design a two-line chart in your spreadsheet app of choice.** I know what you're thinking: *A spreadsheet, gah!* Don't worry, though; this one's pretty simple. Create a chart that has two lines on it. The first line is your "pace" line—I put the number of words I'll need to write each week to hit my target word count by the date the book is due. If I need to write 70,000 words in one year, that equals 1,347 words a week. This is the number my pace line goes up by each week. The pace line is always linear, going from the bottom left corner of the chart to the top right. The second line on your spreadsheet is your actual progress—which you update every day, every week, or at the interval of your choosing. This chart lets you compare your actual pace with your target pace at any moment in time, so you can see whether you're on track to achieve your long-term goal. (If you're not into spreadsheets, I've uploaded a template that you can use to track your own cumulative progress to the website for this book: chrisbailey .com/intentional.)

3. **Track and monitor your progress.** I typically update the chart every week or two, alongside my goal review. For goals I make steady progress on over time—where progress is linear—I typically like to get ahead of my pace line a bit, in case any unexpected obstacles arise. It's also helpful to have a bit more

flexibility with how you'll spend your time, attention, and energy. Sometimes tracking goal timelines serves as a nice nudge for when we need to *pick up* the pace. After all, we don't want to create more work for our future self to do—the self who will have about as much energy to take action as we do now.

Here's what the spreadsheet roughly looks like:

Charting Your Rate of Progress

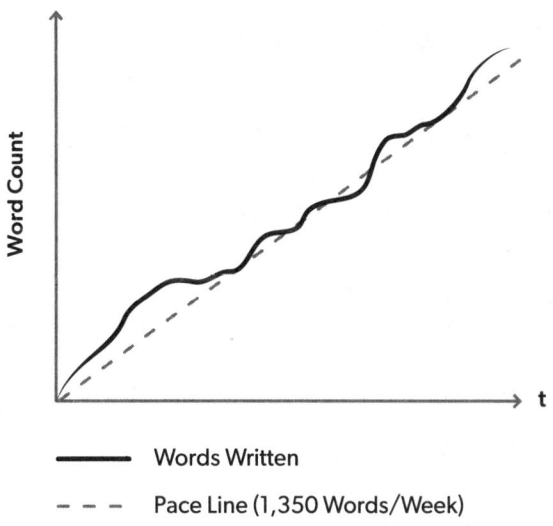

——— Words Written

– – – Pace Line (1,350 Words/Week)

I personally also find that this strategy keeps me honest with myself. I'll typically print a new and updated rate of progress chart every week or two and stick it up in my office where I can see it regularly throughout the day—and where my wife can see it, too, so she can keep me accountable.

Set Milestones for the Near Future

On top of tracking your pace of goal attainment, you might consider nesting a *second* outcome goal that takes place over a significantly shorter time frame inside your original goal—so that it resides farther down the Intention Stack while still being tangible to you. For example, if you have a goal of paying off your mortgage early, inside your goal to "save an extra $2,500 to put toward the mortgage this year," you might aim to "find ways to save $200 this month by reviewing subscriptions and unnecessary purchases."

You can also define a few milestones that you'll hit—and reward yourself for—as you strive toward your goal. For example, if you're writing a company handbook, in addition to tracking your progress over time, you could reward yourself for hitting word count milestones along the way. If your target word count for the book is 10,000 words, at 2,500 words you can treat yourself to a trip to the local spa—if only to get your mind off writing the handbook—and then define subsequent rewards for the milestones to come. (In my opinion, maintenance goals are underrated—consider adding one or two to your list so you can lock in your progress and maintain your most important habits.)

If you break down a long-term goal into either a pace chart or into separate milestones, consider adding a dash of accountability to your plan as well. If you're writing a book, can you give someone you trust—who you also don't want to let down—access to your spreadsheet so they can track how well you're performing relative to your ideal pace? Can you work with your spouse or a close friend to introduce rewards or punishments for following through or not following through with your goals?

When a goal exists far out into the future, the trick is to do what you can to bring the goal closer to you in time—like by tracking your progress or the milestones you hit along the way. Be sure to reinforce your progress with feedback, rewards, and accountability. By doing so, you'll also be able to further lock in your progress, while moving your goals farther down the Intention Stack so they become more attainable to you.

As an added bonus, because you'll be making your goals less aversive, you'll also find that you procrastinate significantly less often.

CREATING A STRONGER STRUCTURE

Something you should know about my wife, Ardyn, and me is that we're both enormous dorks. For example, we have a spreadsheet that tracks the hundreds of games of cribbage we've played together. (The sheet also calculates, with statistical significance, who is a better player. For the record, I'll proudly state that I am—though she programmed the spreadsheet, so she may actually be the smart one.) We also have a spreadsheet to calculate who has done the most chores lately—which also determines how clean the house currently is—so we can make sure the household chores are split fairly between us over time.* On top of this stuff, we diligently track our monthly spending, to both minimize "lifestyle creep" (when our spending habits inflate to meet our income) and make sure we are working toward our joint financial goals.

A few years back, I set a new postpandemic goal for myself: to lose enough weight to get to 15 percent body fat. (My pandemic experience involved a lot of takeout.) Whenever I had set similar goals in

---

*I'll upload a template for this to the book website as well—at chrisbailey.com/inten tional—though you probably don't want it.

the past, I typically had willed them into existence through sheer determination and willpower. So this time, I made a plan to use what I was learning about goal attainment—and doubled down on how structured the goal was.

With my initial outcome goal to lose body fat, I first set a learning process goal: to do research into what exact processes would lead to the greatest progress. For my own goals and biology, I then figured (a whopping) *four* process goals that would serve me best:

1. Operate at a slight calorie deficit each day, to lose fat slowly over time.

2. Continue with my regular strength-training routine, to minimize muscle loss while losing weight.

3. Consume enough protein each day.

4. Get at least seven thousand steps every day (not as much as we *should* be getting, but more than I was getting at the time with my work-from-home lifestyle).

I should say that it took some experimentation—and also quite a bit of research, even after I started making progress—to accomplish these goals. But these were the ones that would carry me through the finish line.

At the start, my motivation was high, but I figured that this would wane over time, as it does with most goals. When it did, I didn't want to let this initial motivational energy turn back into motivational flab. So I doubled down on structure—an incredibly powerful technique for goal attainment, especially with aversive goals. My aim was to give myself *no choice* but to follow through with my fat-loss goal, as well as with its associated intentions. I worked this new goal into a structure I already had in my life: our nerdy joint budget spreadsheet.

As part of our monthly budgeting, my wife and I have both a joint budget and personal budgets, where we give ourselves a certain amount of money to spend each month. To tie this new goal to the existing structure of the spreadsheet, I came up with a simple plan: Make it so I had to "unlock" my personal budget by following through with my fitness goals. I came up with an idea of "fit points" to help me accomplish this. In one late-night sprint of spreadsheet nerdiness, I redesigned my own personal budget sheet so that, if I wanted to spend any money, I had to achieve my health goals for the day: the daily calorie deficit, adequate protein intake, seven thousand steps, and strength training at least three times a week.

To account for the unpleasantness and frustration characteristics of aversion, I made it so the most aversive process goals came with the greatest rewards. I released seven dollars of my personal budget for coming in under the daily calorie budget (and tracking my calories, which I initially found to be a huge pain). I also got three dollars for hitting my daily step count, two dollars for having done strength training at least three times in the last seven days (this took forever to program), and a dollar for weighing myself that day. I didn't have to do all these things every day—I didn't have to do *anything* if I didn't want to—but how much of my monthly budget I allowed myself to spend was determined by the extent to which I invested in these new habits. I asked my wife to hold me accountable for sticking with the sheet, to lock myself into the goal further.

The system worked. And it worked surprisingly well. In the past, I had lost weight by forcing myself, through sheer willpower, to follow through with habits that would become only more aversive with time.

This new system, on the other hand, was built around structure—and better yet, it was tied to an existing structure in my life, my personal budget. If I wanted to do so much as grab coffee with a friend or try a monthly Japanese snack subscription box, I had to do the work and unlock the money first. As the experiment went on, I introduced penalties with Ardyn for my not following through with my goals, like paying her a fine if I didn't follow the system. (She loved this.)

Steadily, over time, I shed the weight. A few pounds lighter, my energy rose. And the fit-point system faded into the background of my everyday life even further—to the point that tracking my daily calories became less of a chore and more of an opportunity to claim the rewards I had chosen ahead of time. A few pounds lighter still, I revised the system, as certain rewards became more and less aversive. My relationship with takeout also changed: It was no longer something I just spent money on but a genuine treat that I enjoyed while following through with my healthy habits. Even as I write these words, the changes have stuck, and I've transitioned into "maintenance mode" with the goal.

Because the structure of the goal was so integrated into my life, change was frictionless. Doubling down on structure worked. And it can work for you, too. Truly. You don't even need to code a spreadsheet to make it happen.

If you find that one of your goals is aversive because it is unstructured, there are a few ideas related to this story (and some that aren't) that you may find helpful.

Plan It Out

First, set a learning-type process goal to discover the best possible process goal (or goals) for what you want to achieve. Structuring a plan to follow through with your goal while your motivation is high works wonders for goal attainment later on, because you'll be able to lock yourself into a goal by developing a system that gives you no choice but to achieve it. It takes some planning for how to personalize a goal to fit cleanly within the existing structures of your life. But it's well worth your while. You'll make that time back in the results you will get.

There are diminishing marginal returns to the time we spend planning our goals: At a certain point, planning hurts more than it helps, because it cuts into your time to actually make progress. Generally, however, we plan too little and not too much. But do keep in mind that if you have the propensity to overanalyze how you will act, too much planning can be as costly as too little. Planning should support your work, not get in the way of it.

Connect Goals to Habits

Once you've structured your goal, consider connecting it with a system or habit you have already. You may not have some overly complex spreadsheet where you track how much money you spend every month, but you do have existing habits that you can tie your new intention to. This "habit stacking"—where you do your new intentions before or after your existing habits—can lower the energy that you will need to achieve your goals. For example, if you're starting a new skin care regimen, try stacking the new habit with another evening habit, like after making a cup of herbal tea or brushing your teeth. Or, if you have the goal of developing a journaling practice, try writing during your train ride home at the end of the workday.

Add Rewards and Penalties

Third, if your goal is particularly complex—or if there's one intention on your list that's significantly more involved than the others—consider doubling down on how structured the goal is, in any way that you can. Try to make rewards, and the occasional penalty, a part of the structure—and involve other people if you can.

One way to do this is to create "habit points." This idea is simple: You pick a few process goals you want to reward yourself for doing—like meditating, saying no to an unimportant work project, or reading. Then, pick a few indulgences—a TV show marathon, time on social media, or treating yourself in some other way. Reward yourself with habit points for following through with your goals. Maybe you'll give yourself 2 points for going to the gym, 1 point for each ten minutes of meditation you do, and 1 point for each random act of kindness you perform. Then, you can redeem these points for the habits you want to limit—but still indulge in every so often. For example, maybe one alcoholic drink costs you 5 points, a massage or manicure might cost 20, and a take out order for dinner might set you back 25.

Habit points reframe vices as rewards, limit how often you indulge, make your positive habits more attractive, and let you strike a balance you're happy with between achieving your goals and indulging along the way. (Be sure to edit over time.)

When you're deciding on indulgences, be sure to look to your strongest values for inspiration. For example, if two of your deeply held values are hedonism and self-direction, a great reward might be a trip to a day spa, where you can move among saunas, pools, and lounge areas as you please.

There are other ways to add more structure to your goals as well. Time blocking when you'll follow through with them, as you do your weekly intention ritual, for example, can be helpful. As can setting a few daily intentions for your personal life that feed into your personal goals. We'll cover these ideas in chapter 7.

TYING INTENTIONS TO HABITS

One more tactic for adding structure to your ugly goals: *Make them more specific.*

Not every goal and intention you set has to be specific to be effective. This is especially true with goals you're drawn to do or are confident you will follow through with. To pick a ridiculous example, let's say you have a goal of eating a chocolate bar every day for a month. You're unlikely to experience a lot of obstacles or aversion with this one. Your level of desire will stay high (assuming you still like chocolate bars by the end), and you probably also won't need to define the goal too clearly.

Other goals that are both aversive and challenging—say, to *stop* eating a chocolate bar every day—benefit from being defined more specifically. Research conducted by renowned psychologist Peter Gollwitzer has found that we "are more likely to attain challenging goals when they are spelled out in specific terms." Conversely, our achievement rates "of moderately specific goals or challenging but vague goals (so-called *do your best goals*) are much lower."[17]

We've already made our goals more specific by defining our process goals. Now, let's talk about making the intentions we set for our goals more specific as well. **The less you want to do something, the more specific you should make your intentions.**

There are three things to define for intentions you don't want to do: when, where, and how you'll do them. When you plan your day and week, defining these things takes a bit of extra effort and time. But aversive intentions and goals also benefit greatly from this planning—and you'll get this time back in spades.

Gollwitzer refers to these specific plans as "**implementation intentions**," and they're how we will actually implement the intentions we set. When setting an implementation intention, we essentially tie an intention to something that will inevitably happen. So, when we encounter the thing that will happen, we follow through with our intention. For example, if our intention is to go for a run, we can make it more specific by deciding we'll go for a run after we wake up. If our intention is to stop scrolling social media during work, we decide to flip on a distractions blocker when we notice we've gotten distracted for the first time.

In a way, setting an implementation intention infuses an intention with some "habit energy." By choosing a certain condition, event, or habit cue in our life to tie an intention to—a time, place, preceding event, emotional state, or the presence of certain people—we create a predetermined response in our mind that we become far more likely to follow through with. According to Gollwitzer, "Implementation intentions create a strong associative link between the specified critical situation in the if-part of the plan and the goal-directed response specified in the then-part." Creating this link means we can act on our intention "immediately, efficiently. . . , and without requiring a further conscious intent."[18]

When it comes to our most aversive intentions, even *defining* how we will act may prove aversive. Remember, though: We need to spend more time than we do planning out our goals—this can save us time in the long run. Research supports that implementation intentions are worth the time investment required—they make us significantly more likely to achieve our most aversive goals.[19] You don't need to set an implementation intention for every goal—or even most of them. But do keep this tactic in your back pocket when you are following through with your most aversive, challenging goals on a daily basis.

The tactic makes following through with your goals far more likely—and automatic. As I hope you'll find, structure can prove an enormously helpful ingredient for following through with your goals and intentions. When you structure a goal right, you give yourself no choice but to achieve it.

THE VALUE OF MEANING

Editing our goals increases how much we enjoy them and makes them significantly more meaningful. This counteracts the last trigger on the list of reasons we procrastinate—meaningless tasks. By knowing your values, and editing your goals to make them more in line with them over time, your intentions become far more meaningful. You'll only move closer to your values as you perform further edits over the timeline of goal attainment.

Values edits align your goals with your true motivational nature, which obliterates much of the aversion you have to following through on them. Eventually, you will get to the point where your goal feels natural, a part of your identity and an extension of who you are. Meaning is a subject we dug deep into in chapter 2, so we won't explore it in depth here. In the context of aversion and procrastination, though, it's worth noting that **it is pretty much always possible to make your goals more meaningful**. This is true even for goals that feel aversive precisely because of their lack of meaning.

To pick a somewhat extreme example, let's say you feel a sense of aversion (and dread) every day you go into work, but you're one year away from retirement and feel that you need, begrudgingly, to "put in the time" before your pension kicks in. "Put in the time" is not a motivating goal for most of us—including maybe for those of us whose top value is conformity. Even in this scenario, we can try on different goals for size to find the one that maps on top of our values the most. Say that you most strongly value benevolence and self-direction (which are combining to contribute to your level of aversion). One solution could be to set a goal to spend your remaining time at work mentoring your colleagues to help them succeed. This shifts the goal from being individualistic to one that connects with your value of benevolence. Another option could be to work within the constraints of your role to exercise self-direction wherever you can, like by choosing which projects to take on—or, if your level of autonomy is low, optimizing your existing workflows.

It is almost always possible for us to reframe our goals so that they become more in line with our values.

If one or two of your goals feel meaningless, remember to give them a needed edit so they become aligned with what you value— and who you are. Often, we must try out a few different goals to find the one we most closely connect with.

AVERSION IS AN INVITATION

Even if your work fires you up because it's important, meaningful, and makes a contribution to the world, chances are some of what's on your plate is aversive: some combination of boring, unpleasant, frustrating, far away, unstructured, and lacking in meaning. Fortunately, with the help of the ideas we covered in this chapter, making good on aversive goals is a *skill* you can get better at over time.

Let the fact that you are procrastinating on a goal be a cue to discover why a goal is aversive and make a plan to follow through more often. The more aversive the goal, the more these ideas will help.

Maybe you need more structure around your goal. Maybe the goal is better framed as a learning goal rather than a high-pressure performance goal. Maybe it's not fun enough, so you should step back to find a way to make the time you spend on the goal more enjoyable. Maybe on a bit of reflection, the goal is too *easy*, and you need to up how challenging it is in order to make yourself actually care. Or maybe you just need to grab your notepad to do a bit of journaling about why the task is so aversive—to connect with the deeper reasons you're doing it and to reflect on the costs of putting it off further.

My challenge to you is to pick a strategy or two for making greater progress on your largest, most aversive goals. As time marches forward—and you make a habit out of counterbalancing the aversion you feel—you'll find the intentions on your list become increasingly effortless, that procrastinating becomes less likely. Putting a little effort in to make your goals less aversive can save you significant energy in the long run.

Aversion makes us avoid doing important things. For this reason, it's a force worth counterbalancing.

Fortunately for us, an ounce of forethought can be all we need—the equivalent of an axe sharpening that will save us time in the long run while working wonders for helping us achieve even our most aversive goals.

5

Attractive Goals

INCREASING DESIRE

*"Ultimately, it is the desire,
not the desired, that we love."*
—*Friedrich Nietzsche*[1]

Aversion is not the only thing that each of our goals contains. Every one of our goals also contains *desire*—an ingredient of goal attainment to which we will now turn our attention. Just as aversion is worth taming, desire is worth understanding—and doubling down on. Let me begin with a story.

One of my favorite parts about writing about productivity advice is using myself as a guinea pig: conducting experiments on myself to push on my mental and physical limits. These "experiments" are typically anything but scientific. They only ever involve one participant (me). This means they're not randomized, double-blind, placebo-controlled, or anything else that makes a scientific experiment valid or reliable. On top of all this, they're also highly subjective. But with all these flaws and caveats, they do have one redeeming quality. I find that they invariably lead me to curious lessons about productivity—and about myself. They provide a launching pad of sorts to jump into the actual scientific, peer-reviewed research about a topic.

Over the years, these experiments have spanned the gamut, from purposefully making myself bored for an hour a day for a month (day one involved reading the iTunes "terms and conditions," for example) to using my smartphone for just thirty minutes a day for a month (which was oddly refreshing, and my attention span grew considerably). I have also tried pushing on other limits, like working ninety-hour weeks for a month. Surprisingly, this one completely obliterated my productivity—with knowledge work (generally, work we do with our minds), there is less of a connection between how long we work and how much we accomplish. We must manage our focus and energy, in addition to our time.

Looking back through all these experiments, the most memorable one for me easily was living in complete isolation for ten days. (It's probably worth noting that this one took place before COVID-19, when "everyone was doing it.") For a period of ten days, I lived in our basement, where I had zero exposure to sunlight—and, more crucial, no exposure to other people. The lack of sunlight was draining, but it was easy enough to compensate for with exercise and vitamin D supplements. The most challenging component of the experiment was having no one to talk to or spend time with. It was lonely down there.

I should note that I had plenty of work to do when I was down in the basement. And the first couple days were indeed superproductive—no surprise; there were zero distractions and interruptions to derail my time and attention. Each day felt like a beautiful, clean slate when I could hunker down and get stuff done. The alone time was also pretty refreshing at first. But then, a few days in, the honeymoon period faded. Around this time, as the days dragged on, I began missing the people in my life—quite a lot.

It was then that something unexpected happened. The more I missed others, the more I saw my level of energy and motivation plummet—even as I had plenty of work to get done and deadlines to hit.

It's remarkable how demotivating not having any people around can be—a lesson I hope you are not familiar with. As time began to pass ever more slowly, I began missing not just the deeper relationships in my life but also the everyday interactions: with coffee shop baristas, friendly neighbors waving hello, and strangers passing by on the street. Down in the basement I had a laptop, food, bed, and a dehumidifier that I named Danby, who I became fast friends with. But there were no people.

On the surface, the conditions of the experiment may sound ideal for getting a great amount of work done—and going in, I was sure I'd be able to. In reality, I found that without any people in my days I had very little energy to get things done. I also had essentially zero *desire* to make progress on what was on my plate. Oddly, tasks that I typically loved doing became significantly more aversive. By the end of the ten days, with substantially less energy and focus, I was far less productive than I had been at the start.

This should come as no surprise: Much of what motivates us is other people. Think about it. Most of us are driven to provide for our families and communities, leave the world better than we found it, and just generally help others. Even if you are not inclined toward altruism, you still probably feel energized and engaged after interacting with and connecting with others. It is other people who are the driving force behind so much of what we do. Plus, other people are also who we get to share the fruits of our productivity with.

The scientific research bears all this out—especially on the motivation front. To return to the motivational bedrock that we all share—the twelve fundamental human values—notice that half of those values are centered around other people. The twelve values live on a continuum alongside one another, and there are a few factors that influence where the individual values fall on the continuum.

One primary factor is that some values are *social* while others are *individual*.

SOCIAL VALUES	INDIVIDUAL VALUES
Conformity	Power
Humility	Face
Tradition	Achievement
Benevolence	Pleasure
Universalism	Stimulation
	Self-direction

Curiously, the value of security is both social and individual, because it includes both personal security and societal security.

In the basement, I had zero opportunity to invest in any of these social values, which made my level of motivation plummet.

On top of needing to muster motivation to get even simpler things done, my overall level of desire to be productive also sank. The same tasks that I originally got excited by became aversive as they became far less desirable. Including writing and connecting ideas—activities that I usually find compelling and inspiring.

So what gives? And more generally, what is it that leads us to want progress on our goals?

Fortunately for us, just as there's science behind what leads us to find tasks aversive, there's science behind desire as well—and how we can motivate ourselves to action. People are a big part of the equation, as you'd expect—and so is how we relate to our goals in the first place.

Let's dig into it.

THE ANTECEDENTS OF DESIRE

One of the most interesting theories related to goal attainment I encountered while researching this book is the "model of goal-directed behavior," created by professors Marco Perugini at the University of Milano-Bicocca and Richard Bagozzi at the University of Michigan.[2] (To give credit where it is due, the theory is built on top of the seminal "theory of planned behavior," which was conceptualized by Icek Ajzen, a professor at the University of Massachusetts Amherst.[3])

The model of goal-directed behavior states that there are five factors that determine how much we desire making progress on our goals in the moment. Let's call these the *antecedents of desire*:

1. The **social norms** that surround us and our goals, which include the social pressure we have either to do or not do something. Regardless of whether we notice this social pressure, it is something we constantly experience, often in the form of "social contagion"— which is when we adopt the intentions of others as our own default intentions.

2. Whether or not something has become a **habit**. If we have already adopted a habit or default intention, we're obviously more likely to follow through with it.

3. How much **control** we have over when, where, and how we will act on a goal. This variable is also a reflection of our past experiences with similar goals, and whether we anticipate that there are any obstacles we will need to overcome.

4. The **attitudes** we have about a goal—whether we think about a goal favorably or unfavorably. This is informed in large part by our values.

5. The **expected emotions** we have related to a goal. More specifically, the emotions or feelings we have about both accomplishment and failure. These emotions drive us toward action and away from failure, and contribute to the level of desire we have about a goal.

As you can see, desire is a function of both yearning and realism. We must *want* to achieve our goals—which the variables of attitudes and expected emotions account for. But for our desire to be strong, there must also be a path for us to follow through—which social norms, habit, and control help pave the way toward.

The overall level of desire we have about our goals leads us to set certain intentions over others, while making our existing intentions stronger. The more we desire a goal, the more naturally we will work to achieve it.

In each moment, in determining how we will act, we will always subconsciously weigh these five antecedents of desire against the characteristics of aversion. (For this reason, there is also some overlap among the characteristics of both—like with control.) Our desire, minus our aversion, creates our overall level of motivation to follow through with a goal. It is through this process that we determine how we will act in ways large and small—to accomplish everything from tying our shoelaces in the morning to saving more money for retirement.

Let's go through each antecedent one by one.

SOCIALLY CONTAGIOUS INTENTIONS

Picking up where we left off with chatting about social desire, the first antecedent of desire—the people who we surround ourselves with—is remarkably powerful. So powerful, it turns out, that it influences both our automatic and deliberate intentions—and therefore motivates us to act in ways that we often aren't even aware of.

Imagine you grew up in a household where you learned that taking good care of your body and mind is more important than pretty much any other priority you could have. Because you were raised in this social environment, as an adult, you may still have a lot of the same default intentions you did as a kid: to notice when you're full so you can stop eating, leave the car at the far end of the parking lot to get some extra steps in, and always defend your evening hours so you get a full night's sleep.

Following a large promotion at work (think, double the salary), you pack up to relocate to a new city with a brand-new set of colleagues. It's a big adjustment. And with new social environments come new social norms—alongside new shared experiences—sometimes for better and sometimes for worse.[4] Say that in this new environment your colleagues don't take good care of themselves, to put it mildly. Working long hours at a grueling pace, they stress eat, stay out late at the bar after work, and don't worry as much about sleep as they do about hustling their way to the next promotion. Over time, even with all the pristine automatic, conditioned intentions you've picked up in the past, you may slowly find yourself edging toward a new set of habits that are less than healthy. The new habits might even go against the grain of your default intentions, and possibly even one or two of your top values.

The behavior of others is contagious—the social norms around us often lead us to adopt new and different default intentions from the ones we already have.

You may be familiar with the notion that we are the average of the five people we spend the most time with. This is social contagion at work. But both fortunately and unfortunately for us, this contagion goes well beyond just five people, to pretty much everyone we know and are in regular contact with.

Let's return to the common goal that 45 percent of us share—to lose some amount of weight.

Because of social contagion, it's difficult to lose weight when we surround ourselves with those who have habits counterproductive to this goal. One study published in *The New England Journal of Medicine* examined the condition of obesity in participants who the famous Framingham Heart Study assessed over thirty-two years. It found a remarkable relationship between how much weight we gain and the people we surround ourselves with. If a friend of yours becomes obese, you become *45 percent more likely* to gain weight over the next two to four years.[5] This is pretty remarkable: We pick up the habits of those around us without so much as realizing it.

The effect doesn't stop with our own friends, though. **Social contagion is so strong that it works even when you don't know the person.** If a friend *of your friend* becomes obese, your likelihood of gaining weight *still* goes up by 20 percent. And, once you go *three* levels deep—in other words, if a friend of your friend of your friend becomes obese—your chances of gaining weight *still* go up by 10 percent.

Researchers Nicholas Christakis and James Fowler, who published this paper, also looked at the social contagion effects of smoking.[6] The same effects hold true here, only they're stronger. If a friend of yours smokes, you're 61 percent more likely to be a smoker. As with obesity, smoking is a highly contagious habit, and the habit cascades much the same way through our social networks. If a friend of your friend smokes, you become 29 percent more likely to do so. Three levels deep, you're still 11 percent more likely.

Numerical stats like these often aren't that compelling—despite the powerful social effect they highlight. To illustrate these figures in a more practical way, imagine a new neighbor moves in next door to you. You *click* with them pretty much instantly: You both have similar interests, can talk effortlessly for hours, and become very fast friends. While you hope your new neighbor never moves away, they do have a couple bad habits they've been trying to kick since before you met them. They smoke the odd cigarette and have some extra weight they've been trying to lose. In a case such as this, your odds of gaining weight and starting a smoking habit just went up *45 percent* and *61 percent*, respectively. These numbers seem unbelievable. Yet the research supports just how influential social contagion can be. Cause and effect can be difficult to weed out from network-based studies like this, but the lesson holds, that the relationship between our own habits and the habits of our friends is profound.[*] [7]

Over time, the effects of social contagion can prove profound in helping us or harming us in attaining our goals. So many of the intentions we set by default are because of the social circumstances we've encountered over the course of our lives.

With every goal on your list, you regularly experience some amount of both positive and negative social contagion that pulls you closer to or repels you further away from your goals. While some of this social influence is overt and obvious, much of it, if not more, may be hidden from your view. It's worth considering how this contagion may be hindering you—but also how it can help you.

---

[*] Curiously, the reason these cause-and-effect relationships are difficult to untangle is because of a phenomenon called *homophily*—which is our tendency to socialize with those familiar to ourselves. Homophily and social contagion tend to get tangled up with each other—especially given that social contagion is driven by shared experiences and feelings.

So how can we become more intentional about using social contagion for good?

One extreme line of advice some productivity experts give involving social norms and contagion centers around auditing every person we regularly spend time with, so we surround ourselves only with people who make us better in some way or help us achieve more. While this advice may be well intentioned, it's simply unrealistic (not to mention more than a little cold and mean). It's also ultimately an approach that prioritizes achievement above all other values—which in practice can prove a costly overcorrection that ends up taking meaning from our lives, not adding to it.

The last thing I'm going to do is suggest you ditch any of your friends that have habits you don't want to "catch." We're hardwired to be social. Having strong social relationships gives us life—not to mention deeper, more meaningful reasons for taking action and staying motivated. Even if we surround ourselves with people who have bad habits, the very act of spending time with them may also support our goals because time with others gives us more energy.

In my own experimentation, I've found the most helpful way to manage for social contagion is to approach it from two angles. We should **understand the negative social contagion** that we unwittingly experience, which is counterproductive to our goals. We should also **double down on the positive social contagion** that can support our goals and lead us to desire them more.

Minding Negative Contagion

Let's start with the negative (yay!). If you've been trying but struggling to achieve an intention on your list, it's worth reflecting on whether certain contagious norms are guiding your behavior in ways you haven't yet realized. Just ask: *Who do I spend time with who has habits counterproductive to this goal?* Reflect on whether you've picked up any of these socially contagious habits without realizing it.

Reflect also on whether any of the people you surround yourself with might feel negatively about any of the goals you're trying to achieve. One way to measure how strong the "social norms" antecedent of desire is for your goal is to "list the three most important persons for you and indicate how much each of them would approve or disapprove." (Verbatim, this is the prompt used to measure this in the original research paper introducing the model of goal-directed behavior.)[8]

Sometimes, even when others don't have contagious habits that work against our intentions, they can have attitudes that go against the grain of the goals we have set. If you have an intention to eat plant-based and your friend group loves to gather around the barbecue when summertime rolls around, you'll experience greater headwinds than if your friends are plant-eating vegans. The attitudes that people have about our goals matter and strongly influence our overall level of desire.

As with a lot of productivity advice, **awareness is key when it comes to understanding social contagion.** Sometimes, the habits you're picking up from others will make you uncomfortable, and you'll want to limit who you spend time with to those more like who you wish to become. Other times, you may find that awareness is enough. For example, I find that I come from a family of fast eaters and that I'll invariably eat more when I'm visiting relatives. A bit of extra awareness is typically enough to remind me to slow down and eat more mindfully.

As we practice awareness, we tap into our self-reflective capacity, which makes it easier to change course. (The one exception to eating quickly for me is when I'm eating some of my mom's dessert that she calls "almond roca," during which it is not physically possible to slow down.*)

Embracing Positive Contagion

Of course, in addition to social norms and contagion leading us to unsavory habits, they can also have the reverse effect and accelerate the positive changes we're in the middle of making.

One powerful strategy for bringing positive social contagion into your life is to make a more concerted effort to surround yourself with people who are working toward the same goals as you are. If you have been struggling to form a running habit, consider joining a running club to not only routinize running but also to pick up related good habits automatically. Or, if you're struggling to meditate on a regular basis, partner up with a friend who wants to meditate at the same time as you do each day—this will add structure, social contagion, and a bit of extra accountability to your newfound habit. If you find that your work is stressful, consider who among your friend group is the calmest and go out of your way to spend more time with them, or sign up for a weekly yoga class together. If there's a skill you're trying to develop, like getting better at photography, knitting, or a new language, search for local clubs to join that will support you.

This is simple advice, but it is powerful precisely because of social contagion. Tactics like these will help you desire your goals that much more—often without even trying. You'll likely also pick up on other positive, ancillary habits along the way.

---

*I've uploaded the recipe to the website of this book, chrisbailey.com/intentional. It's pretty simple to make.

REVISITING HABITS

You may find that some intentions on your list have predictable, regular spikes in aversion. Over time, as you continue to regularly invest in these intentions, your level of aversion is likely to decrease. This is because activities you once had to muster the motivation to do will, given enough repetition, become habits. They fade into the bedrock of who you are: your default intentions.

There is a reason that habit is one of the five antecedents of desire. Specifically defined as "*frequency* of past behavior" in the model of goal-directed behavior, habits can be an effective way to remove the mental effort needed to take on tasks that we find aversive. By forming habits around aversive tasks, we make desire more automatic.

If one or two intentions on your list are habits you are in the middle of forming, keep in mind that repetition and regularity are key. Recall the five habit cues from chapter 1: a certain time, place, preceding event, emotional state, or presence of certain people (there's social contagion at work again). When turning a goal into a habit, act toward it at a regular time and place, alongside another preceding habit that is already formed, or with the same people.

Habits may sound like an odd addition to a model about intentional behavior. But if you've been following along, you know that the opposite is true: Our mind forms our default intentions automatically, in response to the five habit cues. Habits have a rightful place in the model, because they are highly predictive of what we will do—and are a result of the intentions we form. Our automatic behavior must be accounted for in any model that describes why we desire to do what we do. (It could be argued that because the model of goal-directed behavior is a model that looks at which of our intentions turn into actions, habit is a variable that is included for completeness, because it accounts for our default intentions in describing where our intentions come from. Acting out a habit is still a goal-directed behavior, even when our intention to follow through with a goal is automatically generated.)

When it comes to understanding how your level of desire and aversion will unfold as you attain your goals, mind what intentions you can turn into habits with enough repetition. This will lead your desire curves to become much more manageable over time—while you bring greater awareness to how your goals will unfold.

REGAINING CONTROL

So far in this chapter we've covered social norms and contagion and how they help us make goals more desirable—and make us more likely to attain them. We've also briefly covered habits once again— the default intentions that sometimes we wish to form and other times we want to weed out of our lives. We turn now to the third antecedent of desire: how much control we have over a goal.

Given that aversion and desire both contribute to how attractive we find a task, there is significant overlap in which strategies are effective for minimizing aversion and maximizing desire. Sense of control is a great illustrator of this.

Thankfully, we've already learned a lot about how to gain control over our goals. In fact, **every tactic in this book is designed to increase your sense of control** by putting you in the driver's seat of attaining your goals. This is a process that begins with awareness. By bringing awareness to your goals—especially through understanding and defining their shape and the values they connect with—you become mindful of all that you're trying to accomplish, and why. You can begin to define how your goals nest inside one another. Goal edit-ing takes this a step further, helping you refine your goals so they're in line with what you actually want to achieve—as you drop ones that aren't worthwhile. Minimizing aversion—including by making goals more challenging, fun, and structured—gets you more involved with the uglier goals you've set, which helps you feel in control. Even with the goals we *don't* have control over, framing what we have to achieve as a learning goal rather than as a performance goal can significantly up our odds of goal attainment. By reframing aversive tasks, we can overcome the aversion characteristics, not only beating back aversion but also increasing desire, again through increasing control.

Sometimes, increasing our sense of control doesn't mean changing our course of action. For example, pursuing a specific outcome via a learning goal instead of a performance goal, we may take the same set of actions. Or, by performing a values edit, our actions may remain the same while our outcome goal changes completely, to become something we are more deeply motivated by. What matters most with the control aspect of desire is our "perceived" behavioral control—not how much control we actually have, but how much we *feel* we have. As is true for many of these tactics, our relationship with a goal mat-ters almost as much as the goal itself. We must feel as though we have enough control to stick to our plan of action.

We can also increase our sense of control *in the moment*. Over the last decade of researching and writing about the topic of productivity, I've found that most helpful advice for this goal fits inside a single, simple lesson: **As you work, always have an intention behind what you're doing—and make sure this intention contributes to some-thing you find important.** This is *far* easier said than done—that's why there's so much productivity advice out there. But there is always a way to regain our grip on our intentions in the moment.

EXAMINING OUR DEFAULT THOUGHTS, ATTITUDES, AND EMOTIONS

The final two antecedents of desire deal directly with our relationship with our goals: our attitudes and expected emotions. To explore these, let's examine what happens in our mind when we consider how our goals make us feel.

When I asked the monk from chapter 1 where intention comes from, he mentioned one place I hadn't yet encountered in the research: **our self-reflective capacity**. As we've learned, this is our ability to look within ourselves to consider the best way to move forward—with our intentions, goals, and the situation at hand. We can also use self-reflective strategies to tap into how we feel about the intentions on our list in a more *intuitive* way, reflecting, in the process, on the attitudes and emotions we have about our goals. In doing so, we more deeply understand why we desire certain goals.

As you will very quickly see, you will have a great number of thoughts related to the goals on your list. Some of your thoughts may include how you should proceed with your goals, which values they best fit with, and the difference they will make in your life and in the lives of others. Other thoughts, like those that revolve around failure and accomplishment, can be more knotty, because they involve our *relationship* with our goals.

Along these lines, it can also be worth reflecting on whether any of the goals on your list are there simply because someone else expects you to achieve them—not because you deeply want them yourself. One or two of your goals may even fit with someone else's definition of success far better than your own.

Recall the values-inspired definition of success in chapter 2: being true to who you are on a fundamental level. While you may be investing in some goals because they benefit others, where possible, pursue things because they're what you actually desire. In this spirit, it's worth noticing your thoughts about success and failure. As one quickly discovers during meditation—and, for that matter, when procrastinating—a lot of thoughts will get in the way of what we truly want.

If you've found that you really connected with the more logical, rational goal-attainment strategies I've shared thus far, you might find the thought of tuning into your inner thoughts and feelings aversive. There's nothing wrong with that. But if this is you, try to recognize that your emotions get in the way of you getting things done—and that they do so constantly. Procrastination, for example, is a purely irrational and emotional impulse; there's no logic embedded in it whatsoever. Desire is also highly emotional—and this is especially the case with the "expected emotions" antecedent.

Meditation, Again

Let's get hippie-dippie for a little bit. If you've read any of my previous work, you'll know that I'm a big fan of meditation—and that there are scientifically validated benefits that come along with this practice. The main reason I meditate is to become more focused and productive, and to get better at piecing together ideas. Without my daily practice, the ideas in this book would probably read like some gobble-dygook mess.

A curious thing about meditation is how the more you meditate, the better you're able to understand your thoughts and where they come from. The desire we have to follow through with the goals on our list is, in large part, made up of the thoughts, attitudes, and expectations we have about our goals. By examining our own thinking about our goals, we better connect with desire, because we are able to actually look at our attitudes and emotions. We can observe the automatic reactions to our goals that take place within our mind, typically beneath the surface of our awareness. This can be illuminating.

The deeper you go into a meditation practice, the more you learn just how many of your thoughts are more of a *reaction* to something that came before. When someone calls your name, you might think (by default), *Who's calling me?* When your phone buzzes, you might think, *I don't have time for this right now, but is it important?* Not every thought is something we deliberately construct. Thoughts like these are more of a conditioned reaction than anything else.

Curiously, a great number of our thoughts are not stand-alones but reactions to a *previous thought* we just had. When we meditate enough, we invariably find that most of our thoughts exist in a chain of thoughts, connected to other thoughts.

As always, it's easiest to illustrate this with an example.

Picture you're in the middle of vacuuming your house and you find that for no obvious or apparent reason your mind brings up some cringeworthy thing you said at the office Christmas party two years ago. On the surface, the reason this thought arises in your mind might make zero sense. If you've been meditating consistently, though, you may be able to piece the chain reaction together better. You'll usually discover that there is a *chain* of thoughts that you can draw back to some external source that led to your thinking about something in that moment.

Maybe your TV was on while you were doing your chores, and it was some home and gardening channel. Noticing this in a passing glance, you (by default) automatically thought about how you still need to weed the flower bed in your backyard. Which led you to think about how you should pick up a new shovel. Which made you think about the comment you made about your colleague "absolutely shoveling" hors d'oeuvres into her mouth at the office Christmas party a couple years back.

Most thoughts—cringeworthy and not—are the result of a similar chain. Some are more random than others. But just as most of our default intentions (habits) are triggered by a cue of some sort, so, too, are many of our thoughts.

With the Christmas party example, without self-reflection, we may clench our fists and cringe an *eesh!* expression—before glancing around to see if our partner in the next room just saw us wincing for seemingly no reason. We might also feel annoyed with our mind for bringing up the memory.

With a deeper self-reflective practice, though, we may be able to untangle the chain of thoughts more skillfully and see that the thought was a default *reaction* that we can pick apart and understand—not something to take so seriously. We might even laugh a little at how reactive our mind can be.

Picking apart every thought like this would get exhausting after a while. But it can be helpful to know that many of our thoughts are a reaction to the cues that came before them rather than something to be taken so seriously.

In this example, it is our self-reflective capacity that leads us to greater wisdom about what is really happening within our mind. We are able to become conscious of our inner world, to learn and understand, and to move forward with clearer judgment and intuition rather than just reflexively reacting to stuff like some flailing inflatable tube. In the moment, we become more intentional—we can understand rather than react to our default thoughts, while learning not to take them so seriously. And we are able to properly connect with how we feel about our goals, with the attitude and expected emotion antecedents of desire.

If you've ever tried meditation, you know that there are countless thoughts that will tug at your attention as you sit. These thoughts pull you away from your immediate intention—to focus on your breath for a period of time.

The more reactive our thoughts are, the more our default thinking will draw us away from intentionally attaining our goals.

The more we connect with how we truly feel about our goals—the intuitive thoughts we have about them that live beneath the automatic thoughts of our mind—the more we connect with our desire.

We also notice and make room for the many thoughts we have that are related to our attitudes and expectations. Noticing more about how we feel about our goals—and everything else—we expand our self-reflective capacity, while connecting with how much we desire our goals in the first place, instead of getting caught up in the default thinking we do about them.

The vacuuming example might be a bit unrealistic in practice: You're probably not practicing mindfulness while vacuuming or observing every thought, navel-gazing at where they came from. Yet, the broader point still stands. Some thoughts we have are a reaction, while others are deeper and more worth listening to. It's crucial that we distinguish between the two. Reactive thoughts are largely noise; deeper thoughts are largely signal.

The more we develop our self-reflective capacity, the more developed our ability to look within ourselves to reflect on our goals and intentions becomes—we no longer simply react to events around us. It also becomes easier to view our goals as predictions, not expectations, because our thoughts obscure our reality less often. As a result, aversion is less likely to metastasize, thought patterns no longer compound on one another and spiral, and we connect with the meaning behind our goals because we notice the values behind them.

Beneath unnecessary thought is where intuition lies: It's always there, just waiting for some room to break through. With a less noisy mind, we're able to connect with this intuitive capacity more often. We see how we actually feel about our goals—not just the automatic thinking we do about them.

If this sounds like fluff to you, know that there's real research here. In one study published in the journal *Cognition*, the study's authors, Annette Bolte and Thomas Goschke, described intuition succinctly, as when "information [is] activated in memory, but not consciously retrieved."[9] In other words, when practicing intuition, we feel compelled to act differently but can't articulate why. The more room thoughts have to break through, the more we can listen to them—and not just react to circumstances around us. Thoughts cascade less often and less-reactive thoughts have room to break through. Taking action on a goal, for instance, we have a clearer knowledge of why we are doing what we're doing.

A Meditation Exercise

Meditation is a powerful way to connect with and develop your self-reflective capacity. In this book, I cover how to meditate only on a surface level.* If you're not familiar with meditation, it is surprisingly simple: You just focus on the details of your breath for an amount

(continued)

---

* If you want to dig deeper, visit chrisbailey.com/meditate. You won't have to sign up for anything; it's really just a guide to help you get started.

of time that you predetermine, and when your mind wanders somewhere else (which it constantly will), you bring it back to the breath. That's it.

Of course, because the breath is so boring, you'll find that your mind *won't* focus on it. A lot of times it will refuse to, and you'll constantly need to refocus on the details of your breath. (That is, if you even get around to meditating at all—it's a highly aversive practice.)

As you consider meditating, your mind will reflexively generate a lot of default thoughts about why you shouldn't: you don't have much time today, other things are more important, those episodes of *Friends* are not going to rewatch themselves, etc. This is the default noise of the mind. The mental resistance we have to doing pretty much anything—as well as our desires—is structured out of default thoughts like these. As with our default intentions, default thoughts are largely a reaction to a set of conditions that preceded them. They are very often not something we truly, intuitively believe. (You shouldn't feel bad about any of this stuff, by the way: It's just the way our brain is built.)

This all leads us to a common myth about the practice. One thing that many believe about meditation is that it's all about *not thinking* and temporarily turning off your mind. This isn't true.

I'm not sure if you've ever tried not to think or to turn off your mind. But if you have, you've probably found that in doing so your mind thinks *more*—not less! Think about when you try to fall asleep after a particularly busy, stressful day. Your mind is still racing as your head hits the pillow. So you yell at it to shut up and let you sleep. This, of course, has the opposite effect. Much of the noise in your head is comprised of reactive, default thoughts, and the only way to "stop the fire" is to stop adding more thoughts into the mix. (Ways to do this include listening to a sleep playlist or noticing your breath.) Yelling at your reactive mind only adds fuel to the fire.

In meditation, you don't shut off your mind. You can't. Instead, you continually bring your attention back to your breath once you notice that your focus has wandered and you've become knotted up in your own thinking again. In the moment, this feels unproductive and, in a way, pointless; it will feel as though meditation isn't working, and you're just wasting your time, focusing on your breath like some dolt. But the opposite is happening. Each time you notice your mind has fallen down a rabbit hole of thought, you gain a bit more awareness of what's going on in your head—and where your mind can take you without your so much as noticing.

It's busy up there. And when the environments we occupy add only more noise to the mix, being able to step aside from thought to just *experience* something— like the breath—is like a calming superpower. If you can focus on the breath, you can focus on pretty much anything. And if you can *enjoy* your breath, you can enjoy pretty much anything. The more you settle your mind through meditation, the clearer your mind becomes. There are fewer default thoughts flying around in it.

(continued)

Most days, we can count on a single hand how many times we catch our mind lost in thought. In a lot of meditation sessions, you'll quickly run out of fingers and toes. It is in this repetition that over time we begin to take our thoughts less seriously. We realize how much of what runs through our head is reactive thinking that happens by default.

Meditation is fundamentally experiential, and so it is something you really have to experience firsthand. When it comes to connecting with desire, too, I think you'll find what I have: that meditation is in a league of its own.

Journaling, Again

If the thought of meditation doesn't appeal to you, there are other helpful ways to tap into this intuitive, self-reflective capacity and connect with the attitudes and emotions you have about your goals. We've actually already talked about a big one: journaling.

In chapter 4, we used journaling as a way to work out why certain goals felt so aversive to us. Like the best self-reflection rituals, journaling helps us step back so we can separate how we really feel about something from the thinking we do about it by default. This helps us connect with both our attitudes about our goals and how we expect to feel when we succeed or fail at them (expectations).

But unlike meditation, in journaling, you make an effort to *connect* with your thoughts rather than to step back from them. You are able to write out, usually in longhand, how you feel about something or what's going on in your mind. Doing so lets you poke and prod at what you're thinking, while seeing your thoughts laid out in front of you.

The practice can be as free-flowing or as structured as you'd like. For example, if you wish to journal about goal attainment, you might try writing using a prompt along the following lines to get started:

- How am I feeling about this goal? What comes to mind when I think about succeeding or failing at it?

- How much aversion—and desire—do I have with this goal?

- What next steps can I take to manage aversion or double down on desire?

- Looking at the future, what will get in the way of my attaining this goal?

- How does this goal connect with what I value? Is there a different frame for this goal, or a different goal entirely, that feels like a more motivating fit for who I am?

- What goals can I form that haven't occurred to me yet?

Regardless of your journaling style of choice—whether as a ritual or as a response to a certain cue, like that you're feeling aversion and putting something off—I recommend giving the practice a shot.

DESIRE, AVERSION, AND THE INTENTION STACK

As we finish this chapter, let's put it all together. Aversion tends to flow upward from our tasks and deliberate intentions to prevent us from working on things in the moment. Taming it allows us to more easily access the bottom of the Intention Stack. Desire, on the other hand, tends to flow from—and allows us to connect to—our values and default intentions. We can visualize this in the stack.

In this illustration, the place between our default and deliberate

The Intention Stack

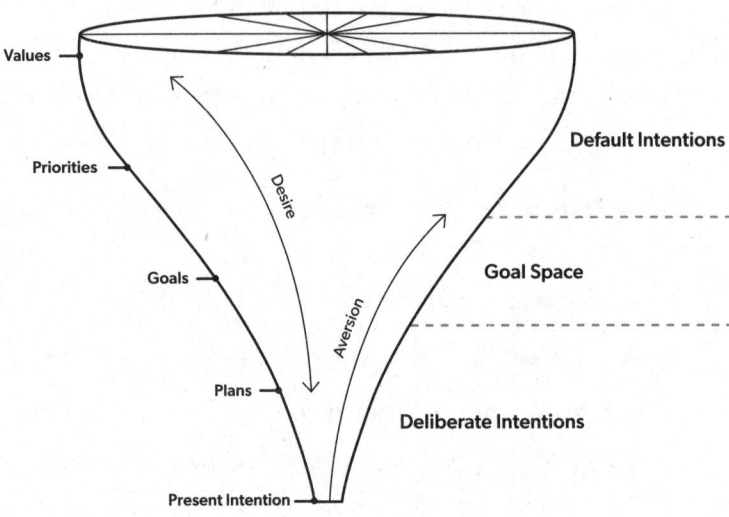

intentions is our "goal space." This is the place from which we aim outward to attain new goals, break existing habits, and align our pursuits with who we are and how we will act. Goals connect with our plans and priorities, which connect with our daily actions and values. This makes our goals a key conduit between our daily actions and values. Along the way, our rates of progress are both accelerated and slowed down by desire and aversion.

For our goals to be strong, both desire and aversion must be accounted for.

Four of the six characteristics of aversion actively prevent us from reaching the bottom: when a goal is *boring, unpleasant, frustrating,* and *unstructured.* The other two characteristics—when a task is *far away in the future* or *meaningless*—are signs that the full Intention Stack has not yet been accounted for. That is, when a task is far away, we have not thought about it for a short enough time span so as to account for the bottom of the Intention Stack. When a goal feels meaningless, that's a sign it isn't connected with our values—in other words, that our intentions at the bottom are out of alignment with our longest-term intentions at the top.

Desire, meanwhile, lets us ascend to the top of the stack. For starters, our values and the default intentions they are made of lead to the *attitudes* we have about our goals. When our attitudes are aligned with our goals, goals become frictionless—they feel natural to do. Similarly, our thoughts, which form our *expected emotions*, lead to even greater alignment. Social norms both influence the default intentions we have in the first place and provide a crucial headwind or tailwind for goal attainment. It is through the *control* antecedent of desire that we account for even more of the stack—control means there is a path for us to actually repel down to the bottom in order to act on what we want. The final antecedent, *habit*, indicates that this path has already been formed, that the default intentions at the top of the stack connect with an action at the bottom. As mentioned earlier, habits are included in the model of goal-directed behavior to account for the intentions we set automatically. While this book is mostly about our volitional actions—and how our deliberate actions fit together in the Intention Stack, a model for volitional behavior—habit still has a rightful place in accounting for desire. Habits determine our default behaviors and desires, the basis on top of which change is made.

Aversion and desire are forces that attract us to or repel us from our goals. And when our goals feel far away, meaningless, outside our control, or against the norms that surround us, this can be a sign that we must account for them in a different way—by considering the entire Intention Stack in our planning.

Regardless of which characteristics of aversion and desire your goals connect with, it's critical to account for both forces on the way to goal attainment.

OVER THE LAST FIVE CHAPTERS, we have explored the Intention Stack—starting at the top with values, then working from the bottom up by talking about process goals (which live near the bottom), outcome goals (which live a bit higher up), and both aversion and desire—which create the room for us to rise even higher and make our goals a priority in daily life.

Now that we have reached the top of the stack once again, it's time to get even more tactical with our values.

6

Deeper Goals

"If you have built castles in the air, your work
need not be lost; that is where they should be.
Now put the foundations under them."

—*Henry David Thoreau*[1]

Thus far in this book, we have covered four fundamental actions essential to goal attainment:

1. Set a goal by defining its process and outcome.

2. Edit the goal so it fits with your life, what you value, and who
   you are.

3. Minimize aversion.

4. Maximize desire.

With each of these steps, we worked our way up the Intention
Stack. We began near the bottom, with the process goals that fed into
our outcome goals (which were higher up the stack). Then, we cleared
a lot of the brush that was getting in the way of our making progress—
through minimizing aversion and maximizing desire.

Now, it's time to once again cover the top of the stack: deepening
our goals so they're even more connected with what we value.

Deep goals are those that connect with our most tightly held values, and when they do connect, they become more than something

we want to achieve—they are an expression of who we are on a fundamental level. They become far more meaningful, and we become more motivated and more likely to achieve them.

When we observe ourselves manifesting our values through our actions, we view what we are doing as much more meaningful and important. Many of us think of meaning (a sense of purpose) in our life as something that is "found." In my view, it isn't found. Meaning is something that is made, constructed. Our intentions and actions become more meaningful to us when we notice that we are expressing our values through them.

Making sure there's a connection between what we do and what we value is not always feasible or realistic, of course. We all have to deal with email. But every one of us has at least a bit of space to make inroads to living in a way that is truer to who we are—at work and at home. The tactics that will be relevant and accessible to you at any time will fluctuate, and that's par for the course. However, at every point do what you can, and your goals and actions will become more meaningful and productive as a result.

Because deep goals are connected with both your values and daily actions, they are a conduit between who you are and how you will act. In this chapter, we'll get tactical, building on the values rituals I've shared already, such as values edits, a key to refining goals so that they become more motivating.

There are countless ways to deepen the goals you have, including by thoughtfully selecting the values you want your goals to contribute to, and making room to invest in your largest values more regularly and deliberately—through intentional indulgence, overcoming guilt, values tracking, values days, and introducing "trip wires."

Let's do this thing.

COMPLETING YOUR GOAL INVENTORY

As we've learned, every goal we have, whether we realize it or not, is connected with our values. Focusing on the bottom of the Intention Stack—processes, outcomes, and priorities—allows you to make greater progress. But your values provide the motivation you need to make this progress in the first place. To deepen your goals, you first have to identify the values each goal falls under.

You may have a bunch of goals you're currently working toward. By now you also may have captured these in a central place you review and edit on a regular basis: your goal inventory (if you need a refresher, head back to chapter 3). Let's build on this.

Because you've already defined your process and outcome goals and have potentially made them more attractive by lowering aversion and increasing desire, the final step is to connect each of your goals with a value that completes the Intention Stack. I do this by writing down which top value (or values) each goal fits into for me.

Value: Health

OUTCOME: **Build a resilient, strong, peaceful mind to support my mental health.**

➡ PROCESS: Meditate for one hour every workday and in the morning with Ardyn.

➡ RATE OF PROGRESS: Fast and steady

OUTCOME: **Build cardiovascular system to support long-term fitness.**

➡ PROCESS: Invest in Couch to 10K program.

➡ RATE OF PROGRESS: Fast

159

Value: Self-direction

OUTCOME: **Create an Overcoming Procrastination course and make it surprisingly delightful.**

➡ **PROCESS:** Solidify course structure and filming details.

➡ **RATE OF PROGRESS:** Medium

This is a simple addition, but it has two big benefits. First, by reminding yourself of the values you are supporting on a regular basis, over time you begin to see your goals and actions as being more meaningful. My goal to create a new course product is nested under self-direction, which frames the goal for me in an even more desirable light: I want to (and get to) be more creative with it and want to take advantage of that (through making it as much fun as possible). This tiny edit makes me more motivated to make progress on my goals in the week ahead. Given that our values are the greatest motivational force in our lives, this has become a powerful weekly nudge for me. I bet it will for you, too.

Second, nesting your goals under your values serves as a small cue to remember to edit your goals so they become even more connected with your values over time. You may also decide to edit the values that your goals are nested underneath, as you find different ones that are a better fit for what you are trying to accomplish.

Maybe one of your outcome goals is to reach complete financial independence so you can retire early. You originally place this goal under the value of self-direction—because reaching the goal will help you choose what to do with your time during the week. In reflecting on your values over time, though, you realize that security is a much stronger value for you—you really want the comfort, stability, and safety that achieving financial freedom will bring more than going your own way. Changing the header in your goals document from Self-direction to Security and writing a short description of how each outcome ties to that value might sound like a minor edit. But each time you review your list of goals, you'll remember what you're working toward—and why what you're working toward is meaningful to you.

ACCEPTING OUR "WRONG" VALUES

Values are our nature. As such, when we don't live in alignment with them, we end up fighting against them. This extends to the cultural values that surround us.

Once you have identified the values in which your goals nest, you may find that some of them may go against the grain of the societal norms that surround you. This holds especially true for goals that contradict Western ideals of success—though any of the values you pursue can feel "wrong" when they are misaligned with the environments you spend time in.

These misalignments lead us to feel needlessly guilty. In most cases, though, this guilt is misplaced—something I found out the hard way with my pleasure/hedonism value.

Intentional Indulgence

While pleasure is a value that many of us share, it is very often misaligned with the environment we find ourselves in.

A tension in my mind about my interest in productivity has always been that I am also, on some level, fundamentally lazy. After a long day, I prefer to relax by lying on the couch—to read or listen to a great book, or listen to a nerdy technology podcast—more often than not with delicious takeout food by my side. It's an experience for the ears and mouth! What's not to love? I don't need beer, stuff for my hair, or fancy clothes. I just need snacks and a good podcast.

My productivity interest and laziness have been living side by side for years. Despite this, I've honestly felt quite a bit of guilt whenever I've invested in being lazy over being productive. Don't get me wrong: It's not that I don't enjoy my lazy time. But guilt usually subtracted from how much I enjoyed the experience. On some level, I felt I was doing something wrong when I was enjoying myself. My level of negative self-talk would invariably spike, just as it might in an episode of procrastinating over an aversive task. Thoughts buzzed around my head about all the better things I could be doing instead:

There's so much that needs to be tidied up around the house—why am I still on the couch?

Another episode? Am I sure I've earned this relaxation time?

A bit of guilt is sometimes helpful because it can nudge us to spend our time and attention in ways more congruent with our broader values and ambitions. Guilt is sometimes a sign that we're spending our time on something that is unimportant and that we should be spending our resources better. But here's the thing: If hedonism or pleasure is something you value, it is critical not to let guilt get in the way of indulgence. This lets you enjoy habits that are aligned with your innermost values even more deeply.

In looking through the research on values, I felt a big sense of relief when I encountered hedonism. On some level, it served as validation for how I was spending my time. The enjoyment I got out of indulging after a long day or week was not misplaced. It *had* a place: in the hierarchy of values that made me who I am. The value is a fundamental part of me: I get meaning out of enjoying myself. If you value pleasure, the same is true for you, too.

Once I saw that sensory pleasure is something that brings me a great amount of enjoyment, I started making more of an active effort to reduce the guilt I felt when I was indulging. Sweeping it under a rug wasn't working. So I started indulging more deliberately, practicing what I refer to as intentional indulgence.

I started to carve out specific times in my week when I would practice indulging intentionally and deliberately. (You may prefer to be less structured with the ritual if you don't value self-direction as much as I do.) When I saw that I had an evening free of plans, I made sure to block off the time in my schedule—not so someone wouldn't book a random evening meeting with me but so I could get excited about that evening when I looked through my calendar for the week. Sometimes, I'd build a small list of what I wanted to watch, listen to, and eat. If an exciting episode of a podcast dropped, I'd save it for that evening. If my wife and I were watching a show, we'd reserve the latest episode for that evening, too (here's looking at you, *Great Canadian Baking Show*). I'd also look ahead to what I wanted to order to eat.

This ritual requires a bit of forethought, which you may or may not find worthwhile, depending on your other values. But if you do have guilt around indulging, it is a near surefire way of enjoying yourself more. If you value hedonism or sensory stimulation, I think you'll be surprised by the extent to which your guilt evaporates. If you're like me, the more intentional you become about indulging, the less guilt you will feel. Try anticipating how you'll spend your time, so you have something to look forward to throughout the week—and to make the evening as enjoyable as possible.

Remember: Intention is not just for accomplishing more—it is for accomplishing more of what you want.

Sometimes you may find that temporarily compromising on another value is worthwhile, like if you decide to have a few drinks with friends even though doing so goes against your value of health. But most of the time, you probably don't need to. Taking a luxurious bath instead of indulging in a meal may satisfy your hedonism value just the same.

The key is to strike a balance between what you value most over a longer arc of time.

Selective Stimulation

One subject I get invited to speak to groups about is distraction—including how to lower how distracting and stimulating our environment is to become more focused and productive. We live in an overstimulated, hyperactive world. When we learn to find focus in such an environment, we develop an edge in pretty much all that we do. Focusing more intently, we not only get more done but also get more out of life, because we're present for more of the experiences that comprise our day.

That said, a big part of becoming less distracted is lowering our level of mental stimulation, which is how busy our mind is. This makes focusing on complex tasks far easier. But, somewhat awkwardly, stimulation is also a fundamental human value. If it's a strong value for you, you may not want to eliminate any or all stimulation from your life. Nor should you have to. You shouldn't feel guilty about this value, either.

It ultimately comes down to where your stimulation comes from. If you want to become more productive, it's probably not wise to engage with empty sources of stimulation, like multitasking—which is one of the biggest productivity traps in existence. But if you value stimulation, this can be a trap that's tough to avoid. Multitasking makes us far less productive, although if you like stimulation, it can also be very enjoyable! The more we try to do at once, the more stimulating our work becomes—even though this compromises our focus. (We also can't actually focus on more than one thing at once. Kind of like when you quickly turn the pages of a flip book and it creates an illustration that looks as if it's moving, multitasking provides the *illusion* we're doing more than one thing at once. But we're really just rapidly switching between things.) Each time we redirect our attention, we lose a bit of focus—a part of us is always devoting a bit of attention to what we were just doing. It's no wonder that studies show our work takes around 50 percent longer when we multitask, compared with doing one task from start to completion.[2]

Multitasking is not the only stimulation trap we fall into that compromises our productivity and focus. Take, for example, your phone, work email, or any messaging apps you use. These apps are stimulating—and because they are novel, they lead to the release of dopamine in our brain when we engage with them. This leads us to feel as though pleasure is right around the corner. In the moment, distractions like these are enticing. But when we engage with them repeatedly, they can serve as nothing more than empty sources of stimulation that make focusing difficult. The more stimulated our mind gets by novel distraction, the more difficult it is for us to "come down" to focus on more difficult things. The busier our mind, the tougher mental activity is to tame: More stories fill our mind, and intuition gets crowded out.

Much as if you value hedonism, if you value stimulation, there is absolutely nothing wrong with you. But as with hedonism, it is worth becoming deliberate about your *sources* of stimulation. The digital world may be stimulating, but there's excitement, novelty, change, and challenge to be found elsewhere, too. You don't even have to go skydiving or bungee jumping! There are far more interesting sources of stimulation than apps that will hook into your brain and provide you with empty hits of stimulation just to keep you scrolling. If you're set on spending time in the digital world, try picking up a challenging yet rewarding video game like *Civilization*, or a calming yet engaging one like *Stardew Valley*. In the physical world, consider joining a running club to invest in stimulation and your health at the same time.

Generally speaking, stimulation is one value that it is worth becoming more deliberate about. There's obviously nothing wrong with scrolling through your go-to apps if that's where you want to get your stimulation from. But for our productivity, there are usually better, cleaner-burning sources. Deliberateness is key.

Embracing Conformity

Another value I want to mention briefly is conformity. As with the others, if conformity is something you value, you may sometimes feel out of place in an individualistic Western world. Of course, and at the risk of sounding like a skipping record, our values are worth embracing rather than sweeping under a rug.

However, as you know, there are some values that we naturally adopt because of the dynamics of the groups we occupy. The cultures we're a part of have different customs, norms, and traditions—which create new sets of default intentions that, through social contagion, we can catch. It is possible to catch these habits even when we don't connect with their underlying motivations (and values) highly. For this reason, sometimes, in a rather ironic way, being a conformist in the modern world can feel like an act of rebellion.

Conformity is not just about being obedient: self-discipline, politeness, and even honoring our elders are considered subvalues to conformity as well. But if you find comfort in rules, laws, and obligations, or in simply avoiding upsetting others, then embracing the conformist within you can provide you with a lot of meaning. Rebel against the modern, individualistic world by being a conformist.

Stepping Into Power

Power—the control of or dominance over people and resources—is the final value I want to touch on in this section. Research shows that a couple things are true about the value of power. First, it is not a very popular value overall. And second, it does have an essential place in both the values hierarchy and the groups we're members of.

In the social groups we occupy, power dynamics are a fact of life, because in most groups, there are people who will have a more dominant role. According to sociologist Talcott Parsons, the more differentiated the roles in a group are, the more often that different members of the group must settle into roles of varying levels of power. For example, all else being equal, power will be more of a focus in a company that has more bureaucracy and more levels—because there are more bosses. As Parsons writes, "It is in these processes of the settlement of terms that the opportunity to exercise power arises, and that its significance to goal achievement resides."[3] Some of us will have default intentions that motivate us to assume the more powerful roles in a group. Power dynamics like these exist within most groups, no matter how benevolent they are. In most charities, there is a CEO; in most congregations, there is a priest; in most cities, there is a mayor.

If power is a strong value for you, you will feel an increased level of motivation as you manifest power through your actions. This is worth harnessing. But as with expressing any value, be sure to respect the values of others in the process—not to mention *your* other values, as there is probably a way of expressing them at the same time (including values such as benevolence and universalism).

Given that the power value can involve dominating others, it is a value that should be skillfully practiced, especially because conflicting values, like self-direction, are far more common in others. Mindfulness is key. Mind that those around you likely have values that differ from your own, while also trying to notice and accommodate the values of others—a great skill to develop regardless of what your own values are.

Being able to see through the actions of others to the values that underlie them is practically a superpower for better relating to others. The more aware you become, the more you will develop this skill over time.

No Bad Values

As human beings, there are a whole host of motivations that can propel us forward—some of which will be far more meaningful to you than others. After discovering what values you love the most, do all that you can to enjoy and spend time on them—and minimize the guilt you can feel while doing so.

After reading through the values research, I still truly believe there are no values that are wrong or right. You may disagree, and that's fine, too. Some values will prove more helpful for certain goals—for both ourselves and the groups we're a part of. Valuing achievement is more conducive to career success. Just as valuing universalism is more in line with making the world a better place. And valuing things like hedonism, stimulation, conformity, or even power still allows us to make a contribution to both ourselves and the world around us. Respect your values, and your actions will become more meaningful.

At the end of the day, it is through embracing your values that you will consider your time to have been well spent.

VALUES DAYS: WHEN A TASK DOESN'T ALIGN WITH YOUR VALUES

Pretty much every goal can be edited so that it fits with our top values. But when we don't always have autonomy over our time, not every task in our day will map on top of what we truly care about. This is especially true with smaller daily tasks that are tedious, that just need to get done, like email. But even during periods of time when much of our work is draining, it is possible to strengthen our connection with our values. One simple way to do this is to pair undesirable tasks with values-centric activities—for example, by taking values days.

In my last book, I shared how I reached (and overcame) a clinical state of burnout because of too much travel for work. (Burnout is always the result of unmanaged chronic stress that we repeatedly experience.) On some level, complaining about traveling for work feels like complaining about winning the lottery—I'm lucky I get invited to talk about my work while visiting some interesting places. But as someone who doesn't value stimulation all that highly but does value self-direction a lot, the stress of travel adds up and contributes to feelings of burnout.

In traveling, there is a certain requirement to give up control. The moment you arrive at the airport, you exist at the whim of airline schedules, airport layouts, and customs agents who may or may not be having a good day. The pace is choppy and weird—hours of waiting punctuated by short bursts of stress—whether to get through security or to run from one end of an airport to the other to make a tight connection. There are typically things you have to monitor as well—flight boarding times, how many minutes you've got to make a connection, or which baggage collection area you will need to wait around at. Over time, if you travel a lot, you pick up some tricks: the best places to wait in airports, how to make boarding easier, and where to sit on a plane.* Experience makes traveling easier. But with enough travel, the novelty of flying also wears off quickly: Tactics like these minimize stress, but they often don't maximize how enjoyable travel can be.

In the past, when traveling for work, I tried to mitigate this by minimizing how much time I spent in a place, which had the nice benefit of maximizing how much time I spent at home. This was great in theory, but in practice I usually felt a sort of whiplash. I'd arrive, deliver a talk or do a bit of work thereafter, and then quickly jet off to go home or go on to the next place. While I had more time at home this way, in practice, I was often too exhausted from traveling to be fully present once I was there again. Eventually, I started to schedule a buffer day—either at home or in the city I was visiting—so I could truly decompress. Now, I flip on my autoresponder, disconnect from as much of the digital world as I possibly can, and carve out the time and space I need to take care of the essential things and settle back in.

---

*My biggest traveling tip: Be kind to everyone at the airport who's helping you out. Airport staff deal with stressed-out and rude people pretty much all day long. When you're uncommonly kind to them, you make their day better. There's also the added bonus that people are usually more helpful when you're kind. So even if you aren't motivated to be kind by your benevolence or universalism values, remember that kindness at airports—or anywhere else for that matter—is a serious time-saver.

Over time, working some values research into this ritual, I've come to think of these as values days. For me, they're mostly an opportunity to invest in my value of self-direction while feeling the ground under my feet once again, settling down after having to perform. Because I have plenty of personal stuff to keep up with, the entire ritual happens during work hours—but it's a true day off for me. No meetings, no calls, no email. I wouldn't replace these days with anything.

You can have a values day whenever it makes the most sense for you and your routine. It doesn't even have to be a day. If the most you can muster is a half day, even an hour, that's fine. But when you have to do something that goes against your top values, take some time to do what is congruent with your topmost values; deliberately spend time on what you find most meaningful.

Having a values day is simple:

1. **Choose a chunk of time that you can "block off" in your calendar to spend time on your highest values.** It helps to schedule a values day after a particularly stressful time—like after a big work trip or handing in a large project at work.

2. **Look to your top values and think about how you can structure a day around them.** If your top values are more individualistic, rent a cabin in the woods for a weekend after a weeklong conference where you have to cater to others. Or maybe your top values involve others: Organize a staycation with a few good friends or spend the day volunteering after a period of solo work.

3. **Create the conditions so you can enjoy the day completely.** Flip on your email autoresponder at work, arrange for child care (unless your day involves your family!), and do everything else you have to in order to enjoy your day and protect the time you'll be spending on your values.

As when you invest in certain values society deems "wrong," guilt may arise when you try out the ritual. This is normal. The key is to become more intentional with how you spend your time—so that deliberateness crowds out any guilt that may arise. It's worth also noting that in a lot of cases, the ritual can pay for itself, because it lets you recharge and provides you with more resources for later on. For me, having a values day after travel makes travel sustainable in the long run.* Whatever your top values are, there's a way to accommodate them.

Because of the relationship between values and meaning, values days can also be thought of as "meaning" days. Whether your values involve yourself or other people, or keeping things as they are versus improving them for the better, the more deeply you connect with them, the richer your days will become.

INCREASING YOUR TIME AWARENESS

Your time isn't always yours—and there will likely always be periods when your level of autonomy is lower than you'd like, making certain goals feel more aversive. There will also always be incremental improvements you can make in this regard—regardless of how well you're doing. But if you want to spend more time on what you value, the first step is to understand how much time you're currently spending in each value—so you can make adjustments accordingly. Let's go through some of the ways you can do that.

---

* On this note, if you find traveling for work stressful, you deserve a day off after travel, too. If you're a boss, be sure to give your employees this day off as well—before they need to ask for it. Travel adds stress to people's work and home lives, and a day off afterward counterbalances that.

Time Tracking

You may have gleaned that I'm a pretty big data nerd—and this extends to tracking certain metrics in my work and life. This tracking—whether it be with rates of progress, how we're doing relative to a goal's pace, or our time (the tactic we're discussing now)—is not for everyone. But if you're a data nerd like I am, it's possible to capture incredible data about how much time you already spend on your values. And better yet, it's possible to do this through time tracking—which also happens to be one of the most powerful productivity strategies out there.

Tracking your time is useful because it makes you more aware of how you spend it in the first place. Then you can begin *analyzing* where your time goes every day—for example, by reflecting on what you accomplished or crunching your aggregate numbers on a spreadsheet—and whether that's truly how you want to be spending your time. Maybe it is, maybe it's not. In which case, you might decide to spend more time on certain projects that have more impact than you originally thought or to spend less time distracting yourself throughout the day.

You can take time tracking a step further, to not only track how productive you are but how meaningful your time was, too.

The tactic here is simple: Track your time and, while doing so, write down which top value(s) you are investing in as you do. Remember, there is always a value underlying what you are doing.

As with the best productivity strategies, you more than make back the time you spend tracking in how much more productive and intentional you become.

There are multiple ways to track your time. One way is with a spreadsheet, and I've uploaded a template for this to my website, at chrisbailey.com/intentional. This sheet includes a place to track which top value you're investing in, and I programmed it so that it will show you a summary stat of how much time you spent across your twelve values. Most of the time, our actions are motivated by several values at once. Try to pick the top one—though there's a space for a secondary value as well. (I try to pick just one when I use the sheet.)

Digitally, you can also track your time using an app—there are dozens on dozens of great ones available in your app store of choice. If you do go the app route, try to find one where you can add "tags" to your tasks, so you can label each task according to the values you spend time on.

Of course, you can also track your time the analog way, on a simple sheet of paper. I like to write the hours of the day on the lefthand side of the page and then make a couple columns to house both what I worked on and what value my actions most fed into.

Regardless of which method you choose, it's helpful to break your day into thirty-minute chunks of time, though fifteen-minute chunks work great, too, if you want to get more granular. I personally like to track my time in thirty-minute increments at both work and home (when I am tracking my home time, which I do far less often than with work).

After you track your time, be sure to reflect on the findings: Are you happy with how much time you spent across your values? What improvements could you make to not only deepen your goals but spend even more time on your most important values every day? Remember to take it easy on yourself in the process: Consider how you are spending your time as a starting point for setting further process goals. The fact that you're bringing greater awareness to how aligned you are with your values should be reason enough to pat yourself on the back.

TUESDAY, APRIL 8

	ACTIVITIES	VALUE
9 ___ 9:30	} EMAIL CATCHUP	} CONFORMITY
10	MENTOR MEETING	BENEVOLENCE
10:30 ___ 11	} FEEDBACK MEETING	} ACHIEVEMENT
11:30	BREAK - RUN	SELF-DIRECTION & SECURITY

Some people I know track their time every day, and have for years. I personally don't, but I typically invest in the practice when I find that I'm working more on autopilot in response to what comes my way—or when I'm in the middle of a bunch of projects and want to up my level of time awareness to see where I'm investing in it. I have also found that time tracking pairs well with time blocking (a ritual I'll cover in the next chapter).

Initially, time tracking may give rise to aversion. Many of us feel a high level of resistance to the tedium of tracking every hour of our workday. I challenge you to give it a shot, though. You'll be surprised at how well it works.

Reflective Time Awareness

If you can't imagine time tracking fitting with your workflows and life, it's also possible to increase your level of time awareness in ways that don't involve tracking. The best way to do this is to tap into your self-reflective capacity—whether throughout the day, at the end of the day, or during your weekly goal review.

As I dug deeper into the research on values, I started to see people's decisions and motivations through the lens of values. Maybe by this point, you've also started to think more about your own values and what underlies the actions you take throughout your day—both deliberate and not. Some things we do out of obligation—and conformity. Other times, we have a bit of leeway and choose to go our own way—with self-direction. And sometimes a bunch of values are at play—working toward a project deadline, we can see that conformity, benevolence, and achievement are tangoing with one another behind the scenes of our actions.

Values are everywhere and motivate everyone.

The next time you practice a bit of mindfulness, get curious about the values and motivations driving your default intentions. The shorter the time frame you reflect on, the greater the insights. Tracking your time every fifteen or thirty minutes provides greater, more granular insights than reflecting once at the end of the day. But doing a daily "values reflection" can still be helpful.

One option is to introduce a periodic values reflection into your journaling habit. Reflect on what values you spent time on that day—or since you last journaled. In a habit like this, the most novel parts of your day may stick out above the others, while other periods of the day may feel like a tangled mess that's difficult to unknot. The idea is to get close—and to look at both what's going well and what you can incrementally improve on (including by setting a new outcome or process goal). If you're having trouble recalling your day, look through your calendar, text messages, or photos: This can anchor your mind to recall an earlier time and what happened around it.

Another option is to habit stack a short mental reflection with another habit you have near the end of your day, like brushing your teeth or making dinner. (See "Connect Goals to Habits" in chapter 4 for more on habit stacking.) Even a short pause to recall the day and reflect on which values you invested in can be beneficial.

And as a final suggestion: Use your weekly goal review as an opportunity to reflect on which values you invested in throughout the week. Because time distance warps our perspective, revisit your calendar to remember where the heck your time went. Then, be on the lookout for both what was meaningful and for incremental improvements you can make. Should you want to make any changes, your goal list is right in front of you.

TRIP WIRES: HOW TO MANAGE
CONFLICTING VALUES

As our longest-term intentions, our strongest values can lead to other intentions of all durations of time—all of which nest inside our values at the top of the Intention Stack. This is true even for values that we tend to invest in over shorter durations—like stimulation and hedonism. While we may tend to spend time on values like hedonism in the short run—like by having nights out with friends—these same values can lead to longer-term decisions, too—like a career as a day trader.

These value conflicts are especially apparent when it comes to our impulses—the strong default intentions we have that are usually rooted in our values but are also incredibly short in duration. While enjoyable in the moment, these impulses can prove to be a "net negative" because they lead us to compromise on our deepest goals. We may have the goal of living a long, healthy life, but we also have an impulse to order a freshly made donut with our morning coffee. Or we may desire a calm and focused mind, but in the moment, we want to spend more time doomscrolling through social media (to keep those dopamine hits coming).

Morgan Housel, the author of *The Psychology of Money*, writes that "a lot of financial debates are just people with different time horizons talking over each other."[4] A similar idea echoes true here: So many of our internal conflicts are the result of different *values* talking over each other.

If you have two values that conflict, a great strategy for respecting both is to introduce "trip wires" into your day so you can notice unintentional impulses that you don't want to engage in—even if they technically align with your values. This tactic is particularly helpful given that our impulses happen mostly on autopilot. Trip wires help us insert a "self-reflective loop" so that we can notice what we're about to do, take a breather, and reflect on how we truly want to proceed.

There are a few values that we tend to invest in more impulsively, like hedonism, stimulation, achievement, and power. Luckily, the options for introducing trip wires for impulsive habits nested inside these values are endless.

For hedonism, maybe you have the habit of staying up late to watch TV. As a trip wire, you can put a large plant in front of the TV that you'll have to move if you want to watch. This might help you pause long enough to consider how watching TV fits with *everything* you're trying to accomplish. Or, if you tend to impulsively buy things online, you can try removing the saved credit cards from your phone, so you have to (annoyingly) manually enter the numbers when you want to buy something. Or, better yet, you can set up email spending alerts that get delivered to a partner or trusted friend's email address, having asked them to hold you accountable. (An ounce of prevention is worth a pound of cure.)

With stimulation, let's say you have a habit of impulsively checking social media when you're bored, and that this is something you want to change. If this is you, you can try changing your password—but to something so long and so hard to remember that you'll have to reset your password to access the website or app again. Or maybe you impulsively check your phone when you are out for dinner with your family. In that case, you can try doing a "phone swap" with your partner. That way, you still have a phone to take photos with and you can still be aware of any emergency calls that might come in for one or the other of you. But, you both won't have a personalized hyper-novel world of distraction at your fingertips.

Achievement can also be a value that you invest in impulsively. For example, maybe you have a habit of overcommitting yourself at work or socially. In this case, before taking on something new, you can first ask if you'll need to drop any of your existing commitments to make the new one happen. Or, adopt a "one in, one out" system for commitments if your schedule is already packed full. You can also turn this value around on itself. For example, you can download an app to track your streaks for not engaging with the impulsive habits you want to break—while also tracking your good habits that you want to reward yourself for investing in, or the habits and goals you have already formed that you're in "maintenance mode" with. Like with the phone swap, you can also introduce some extra accountability into the picture by asking a loved one to be your accountability partner with a habit you're trying to break.

It can help for you to introduce a bit of aversion into the picture as well. For example, if your partner is holding you accountable, you can ask them to call you out when they catch you slipping—and introduce a penalty for doing so. Before I was born, when my parents quit smoking, they signed a contract with my aunt that stated that every time they smoked a cigarette, they had to pay her fifty dollars (more than a hundred in today's dollars). They haven't smoked a cigarette since.

Finally, let's talk about power. Say you have a bad habit of dominating conversations. In this case, you can create a rule for yourself, like to let two other people in a group speak before you do. Or maybe you impulsively act out your power value by making impulsive "look at me" purchases of expensive, high-status items, like oversized luxury watches or fancy Birkin handbags. A trip wire for this habit might be to have a "twenty-four-hour rule," where you wait a predetermined amount of time before buying an item—maybe even an amount of time proportionate with how much the item costs—one day for every hundred dollars. This trip wire also works well if you tend to impulsively buy things for stimulation reasons, too.

Regardless of the value an impulse is connected with, when an impulse steers you off course, you can also use the fact that you're getting back on track as a trip wire to deal with the issue. For example, perhaps you have what you consider to be a bad habit of checking the news as you work—which causes you needless stress and anxiety. A trip wire for this habit might be to enable a distractions blocker, like Freedom or RescueTime, to block access to news sites for a while so you can't go there when your impulse kicks in. The very first time you notice that you have veered off course, enable the blocker and don't waste any additional time. (You can configure these to block any problem websites—shopping websites included.)

Our values can be expressed across many different time frames. But that said, just because you don't want to invest in a value impulsively doesn't mean that you can't invest in that same value in some other way. As you consider if you want to introduce any trip wires for your habits, reflect on whether you can satisfy the same value through a different approach. For example, if you value pleasure and typically indulge this sense by spending too much money at the spa, there are countless other ways you can indulge instead. You can luxuriate in sound, by putting on a pair of great headphones and listening to your favorite album. You can engage with taste and touch by cooking one of your favorite meals. You can engage your eyes by enjoying a film with stunning cinematography or soaking in the sunset or the night sky. With touch and smell, you can re-create your favorite scent by purchasing it in essential oil form—and adding that to a bath. The options are endless.

The more you get ahead of your impulses, the more meaning you'll get out of the experience you create for yourself—while you work toward both your short- and long-term goals.

VALUES DON'T SHINE A LIGHT only on who you are—they *are* who you are on a fundamental level.

Know them, invest in them, and connect with them.

You won't just achieve more of your goals. Crucially, you'll find more meaning along the way, too.

7

Intention Rituals

"If one does not know to which port one is
sailing, no wind is favorable."

—*Seneca¹*

ntentions are slippery. The reason for this is similar to why it's so
hard to focus on your breath during meditation. Within mere seconds, your original intention to focus on your breath begins to
fade as you focus on much more novel and compelling things, including the thoughts in your head. And this happens while keeping only
one intention in mind!

When we first set an intention, we hold it front of mind. The intention is crisp, freshly conceived, and, when structured well, propels
us forward into action. But most of our intentions are never as strong
as they are the moment they are set. They quickly begin to wash away
as they come into contact with forces external and internal.

Just think about the New Year's resolutions you have made in the
past. We typically set intentions like these with a great amount of
resolve—to finally make some change to our life. Then, it's a familiar
pattern: This resolve is eroded by internal factors like aversion, a lack
of desire, or not enough forethought. Or it's derailed by external factors, like a lack of resources, emergencies that come up, and other
constraints of life.

(Let's pour one out for the intentions we've dropped along the way.)

Given how slippery intention is, it should be said that there is no perfect strategy—or set of strategies—that will ensure future intentions we set won't share a similar fate. But here's an honest question: Would we even want one? If every moment of our life were perfectly predictable and controllable, life might be kind of . . . boring. The rain on one day makes us grateful for the sun on the next; it's unexpected and novel events that create a contrast that makes our days both memorable and interesting. Losing grip on our intentions as we work and live our life is only natural because, as we've talked about, it's impossible to predict or anticipate how our intentions will interact—or more realistic, collide—with reality. The future is tough to predict.

As we step back from the Intention Stack in this chapter, we'll discuss the tactical ways we can form better, stronger intentions, starting at the bottom of the stack and working our way back up to the top. We'll start small, because shorter-duration intentions are more accessible and tangible: They're easier to make sense of because we set them constantly. Every action you took today, to get to the point where you are now reading this book, was possible because of the many small intentions you set along the way.

ISLANDS OF INTENTION

As I hope you have found throughout much of this book, becoming more intentional is, in practice, a matter of stepping back from autopilot and examining where it is you truly want to go. It's hard to practice intentionality amid the chaos of work and life.

Take work—a context that has been a major focus of this book. Our work is usually a hotbed of activity: Once we get caught up in it, our most important tasks can become indiscernible from anything else. We often settle into an automatic rhythm of doing what's most urgent and most in front of us—while we lose sight of and perspective on what's most important: where we want to go.

This isn't always the case. It is often possible to hold on to deliberateness as we work in a brisk rhythm. But losing grip on our intentions is surprisingly normal: Work is messy, we have a lot going on, and questioning every single thing we spend time on would require significant mental overhead that is better spent on actually making progress. Moment-by-moment deliberateness is not always possible or realistic. Emergencies arise, kids get sick, pets walk in while we're on video calls. Setting deliberate intentions is not always possible.

Yet, the more we act with intention, the more productive we become. We simply work on more important things over the course of the day and consider more often what the most productive and meaningful course of action will be.

Our life is the same way. Maybe at home you're less concerned about being productive and more interested in extracting more meaning out of your time. By stepping back at home, too—whether at the start of the week or as a Sunday morning ritual—you can align your actions with what will be most meaningful to you in the week ahead.

It is through strategically stepping back from our work and life, for even just a few moments, that we can chart the best course forward. We find quiet refuge. Outside the arena of activity, we see the fray for what it is—a limitless buffet of options for how we could be spending our limited time, attention, and energy. With so many options for what we can do—across all the contexts of our life—it is critical that we step back to set intentions for what to do in the first place.

This is the process of working smarter. We quit reacting and get a chance to practice thoughtful intentionality—while working within the constraints of our limited time, energy, attention, and other resources.

The best way I have found to do this is to create islands of intentions: pockets of time where we stop what we're doing and plot the best course forward from quieter ground. These islands can be large or small. You can allot an hour during your weekly goal review, conduct a ten-minute morning intention-setting ritual over a cup of coffee or, smaller still, regroup for five minutes between tasks to decide what to focus on next. We'll cover all these throughout this chapter.

The best intention rituals, including the ones in this chapter, have a few things in common.

First, they help us decide what we *will have accomplished* after we carry out our intentions. In this way, the best rituals help us step into the shoes of our future selves. We should be able to look forward and backward at the same time: looking forward to a specified point in time and then reflecting from that vantage point on the progress we will want to have made by then. In this way, the ritual should serve as a way of biting off a bit of progress—first, in our mind, then through the actions we will take.

Second, rituals should help us do this across multiple time frames. If you have a goal of gaining ten pounds of muscle, a good intention-setting ritual will guide you through deciding how you'll make progress on this goal every day, week, month, and year—in ways that support and flow into one another. So, in choosing how much progress you want to have made today, you can ensure that this rate of progress supports the rate at which you intend to progress this week, month, and year. At the same time, you can ensure that these intentions are nested inside one another where possible.

Third, and finally, the best intention rituals should be *simple*. I wrote earlier about how we should spend more time planning than we already do—especially given that we make this time back in increased goal attainment and productivity. But that said, planning also shouldn't take up too much of our day. We more than make back the time we spend planning, but eventually, we reach a point of diminishing returns, at which time we'd be better off getting actual work done. The best planning rituals support us in achieving our goals, but once they do, they get out of our way and let us get back to work—or, on a personal level, back to living our lives.

Here's a quick reflection exercise that illustrates the power of intention. Right now, ask: What is the most *meaningful* intention you could possibly set in this moment? Or, if you're in a productivity state of mind, what is the most *impactful* intention you could set in this moment? Maybe your answer to either one of these questions is reading this book. Or maybe you have a different answer—in which case, what are you still doing here?

Let's start at the bottom of the Intention Stack by talking about interstitial intention-setting rituals—because these help us become more intentional in the smallest unit of time that we will focus on in this chapter: each moment.

INTERSTITIAL TECHNIQUES

Interstitial intention-setting rituals guide our actions in each moment. When we sprinkle these rituals into our workday, they help us decide what to work on right now—and what we will do next.

Depending on how much you value control, you may feel one of a couple ways about these. If you don't generally procrastinate a lot or your day is largely predefined for you, you may find these rituals unnecessary. But if you do struggle to stay focused on what's important, these rituals can help you stay on track. In some cases, they will feel like total game changers.

Two of my favorite interstitial techniques are to practice sequential productivity and time blocking. These two techniques are substitutes for each other: Each helps us to define the sequence of tasks, actions, and commitments we'll engage with throughout the workday. (They work at home, too, but you may not want to get as rigorous with setting intentions there when you're not in work mode.)

Sequential Productivity

The first technique, sequential productivity, involves always working with two things in mind: the task you're currently supposed to be doing and the specific task you will work on next. I find it helpful to keep both continually noted on a temporary surface of some sort that I'll see throughout the day; I'll typically use either the whiteboard in my office or a plain text note file I keep open in a window as I work on the computer. This way, I can see my next intentions frequently. For example, right now, my list looks like this:

- **Current task**: Write book for ninety-minute focus sprint.
- **Next up:**
  - ➡ Fifteen-minute scatterfocus break.
  - ➡ Respond to email from Nina.
  - ➡ Meet with speaking client.
  - ➡ Define structure for an upcoming talk.

The next tasks are always listed sequentially—you work on them in that order.

As you work, you will veer off the intention constantly. When this happens, and you're reminded of what your current focus *should* be (like when you glance at your list), just decide where you'd like to go from there. Sometimes you may want to update your current intention to be what you veered off course to do. If that's the case, reflect on whether the update you're considering making is truly more important than what you had originally intended to do. (There are times when you'll want to resume working on what you had originally deemed most important.)

The ritual also works wonders because it forces you to focus on tasks sequentially rather than concurrently. In other words, you'll multitask less—and invest more attention into your tasks as a result. You'll accomplish more with the same amount of time.

I find that organizing tasks sequentially works especially well on days when I'm juggling a lot of commitments and want to stay agile but not feel overwhelmed. I can constantly rearrange the next tasks as new things come along or as I reflect more on the relative importance of the task as I work. At the risk of sounding like a broken record, constant realignment is part of the process of goal attainment. Your list of tasks should serve as a cue in your environment of what you should be focusing on. The more you notice your current and next intentions, the more you can redirect toward what's important.

Some days are nice when they're a bit less intentional—when there's some room for the unexpected, whether that means you can accommodate unexpected events, serendipitous opportunities, or an extra scatterfocus break or two to incubate a problem or an idea. Other days, you'll want the extra structure. Ultimately, whether or not you practice this ritual depends on how much structure you'd like on a given day and how much time you're spending thinking about all the other things you have to get done. Take what works.

That said, sequential productivity works especially well for less structured days, when you have fewer meetings and appointments—when you have autonomy with what you will work on and when.

It also works more effectively if you have a "maker's schedule" compared with a "manager's schedule." This distinction, popularized by computer scientist and venture capitalist Paul Graham, is one of my favorite ways to think about how our calendar differs from those of others. The basic idea is that those of us with a maker's schedule have most of our days free for creation—whether that means writing, programming, or illustrating. Managers spend most of their days in meetings. This means that for someone with a manager's schedule, one extra meeting is easy to accommodate—just find a time slot for it. For a maker, though, one extra meeting is far costlier. If they have zero meetings and suddenly one gets scheduled, that'll chop their day up into two halves. This provides far less time to do deep work.

If you're a maker, sequential productivity may be a better fit for the rhythms of your work. If you have more of a manager's schedule, time blocking may be a better fit for you, because it accommodates how much or little autonomous time you have on a given day and doesn't require you to guess at how long things will take.

A few other tips for sequential productivity follow.

- **Keep a "distractions list" as you work on your current task.** When you are focusing on your current task, distractions will arise. You'll feel the sudden urge to pick up your phone to text someone, switch over to a different window to check social media, or instant message a colleague. When this impulse arises, capture the task on your distractions list. This way, you can indulge in it later on, as a reward for finishing your current intention. (If the distraction is important, you may instead decide to capture it on either your list of next tasks or your to-do list.)

- **Don't worry too much about interruptions that are outside your control,** like office visitors or annoying colleagues. These interruptions are a natural offshoot of the fact that you work with other people. Just resume working on your original intention as soon as you're able—and as soon as you become aware that you've veered off the intention.

- **When you veer off the intention,** instead of just updating your current task, use the interruption as an opportunity to reflect on whether what you were originally working on really is important. If it is, noticing this will let you get back on track in a way that will help you increase your level of desire to do the task, because you will remind yourself of its importance. If it isn't, update your list of tasks to be more in line with what's productive. If, when you veer off course, you figure the new task is important but won't take long (a couple minutes), there's no need to update the list—the idea is to stay intentional, not spend more time than necessary managing yourself.

- **It may be worth defining your current and next tasks for certain projects or areas of your work, too**—not just your work in general.

For example, if you're a professor, you may have sequential next steps defined for the areas of research, teaching, and service. If you're a project manager, you may have next steps defined for each of the different projects you're currently managing—so when you change your focus to a new area, you know clearly how to proceed.

Time Blocking

Time blocking is a simple practice: You determine exactly when you will work on your daily tasks, usually at the start of the day, in blocks of time that you then "chunk" your day into. I like to schedule things in thirty-minute blocks and make an effort not to plan to do something for longer than ninety minutes, for reasons I'll get to.

Carving out this time away from work to logically think through your day accomplishes a couple things. First, you get to comprehensively consider all the things you will want to accomplish—this lets you make progress on everything you need to, so nothing slips through the cracks. (It helps to keep your list of work goals nearby when you define your time blocks.) Time blocking also, just as important, provides you with greater confidence that whatever you're working on in the moment is what you *should* be working on. This means you'll experience less doubt as you work, because you will have predetermined that whatever it is that you're spending time on was the best possible thing to be doing.

To make time blocking as effective as possible, what you block time for must be grounded in a deep knowledge of what's important. When it is, you ensure your momentary actions contribute to a larger purpose. Each block of time becomes a brushstroke that paints a picture of what you will accomplish.

Over the last decade of my studying and writing about productivity, time blocking has unfortunately never really stuck for me (until I changed my relationship with the practice). I have always found the technique a bit constraining. As someone whose highest value is self-direction, I like feeling in control and don't like being told what to do. Maybe, weirdly, this extends to being told what to do . . . by myself.

In the past, to time block I would typically chunk the following workday out at the end of the current one—this way, I could loosely think about what I would be spending time on between when I finished work and started the new day. Returning to my desk the following morning, though, my reaction was invariably the same: I'd look at my upcoming day with resentment and dread. Even if plenty of breaks were interspersed between my focus blocks and I was working on stuff I found enjoyable, seeing that most hours of my day were predetermined for me instantly made me feel tired. Instead of feeling as though a day was full of opportunity and promise (along with a few meetings), I saw basically every time block as an *obligation*, determined for me by some previous version of myself. I typically didn't go so far as to rebel against my past self, but I was tempted to. *Screw this guy*, I'd think. *I'll spend my time however I want!*

Just as the same set of actions can help us attain multiple goals, most of my time-blocked and non-time-blocked days probably looked the same. I had things to do and I got them done. What changed was my relationship with my work.

When I was in the planning stages for this book, I knew I needed to write about the practice: Time blocking is a remarkable technique for ensuring your daily actions are guided forward by your overarching goals and intentions. But I also wanted to make the technique work for me: I set out on a mission to figure out a way to time block that helped me accomplish what I'd sought to do—while not feeling as though I was losing autonomy in becoming more intentional. (The irony of this is not lost on me.)

My time-blocking breakthrough came in the form of a rather basic (and, in hindsight, obvious) realization: that I didn't need to schedule my entire day ahead of time, all at once. Time blocking, as it is most commonly practiced, involves scheduling your whole workday as you block off time for different things. To feel more autonomy in the moment, at the start of the day, I still defined how long I'd be working on various tasks. But after defining what I would spend time on, I didn't schedule anything. Instead, as the day went on, I'd choose which time block to start next. Sometimes, I'd choose the next few things to work on; other times, I'd choose just the next one. It was a simple change, but I still experienced the benefits of having predefined what I would spend time on—with the control I wanted.

It took a bit of extra work during the day to block the hours of my day as it went on, but this let me hold on to the feeling of being in control—even if my days would have looked the same either way. At the start of the day, I made a list of all the blocks I wanted to spend time on (and for how long). Over time, I'd come to think of the ritual as "rolling time blocking."

My ritual is an easy one, and I typically like to schedule my day the analog way. In the morning, on the lefthand side of a sheet of paper, I write the hours of the day I'll be working. Then, as the day begins, I'll slot in the first few blocks. And go from there. As the day goes on, I now typically have the next few blocks scheduled. This takes advantage of dedicating long blocks of time for focused work but still gives me the freedom to direct my day. Of course, it's important to make sure you have time free in your calendar to fit those blocks into. If you've tried time blocking your day and the ritual hasn't stuck for you, I highly recommend giving this modification a shot.

As you think about practicing time blocking—or if you already practice it and are looking for ways to up your game—there are a few general rules of thumb I'd recommend following for the practice. (Even if you don't time block, you may find these ideas helpful.)

First, keep your work blocks to a maximum of ninety minutes. As I mentioned earlier, research has shown there's a loose limit to how long we can focus for each day (around four hours). Helpfully, research also shows that our energy moves in predictable rhythms throughout the day—more specifically, in ninety-minute cycles.[2] Throughout the day, we alternate between ninety-minute periods of wakefulness (focus) followed by twenty- to thirty-minute periods of sluggishness (tiredness). For this reason, if you're blocking periods of time to hyperfocus on one task, limit those to ninety minutes, punctuated by refreshing breaks.

Schedule plenty of breaks. When I practice time blocking (as opposed to sequential productivity), I'll always schedule ample breaks throughout the day. The research on the proportion of the day we should be on break for optimal productivity is interesting. Generally speaking, we break for too *little* time, not too much. Recall how you move between periods of wakefulness and sleepiness throughout the day. To work with our body's rhythms, using this same ratio, we should be on break for twenty to thirty minutes for every ninety minutes worked. This equals 18 to 25 percent of the workday.

Other studies support this same work-to-break ratio. Two different studies, conducted by DeskTime (a time-tracking app and blog), found that their most productive users were on break for 20 to 25 percent of the day.[3] This may sound like a high proportion of the day, but I can vouch for it: I break for a quarter of each workday and I find this level works very well for me. This is the rhythm I used to write this book. This is the equivalent to a one-hour lunch, with an hour distributed across the entire day. Remember also that your brain does not stop working when you let your mind wander.

Try time blocking both the analog and digital way. We relate differently to the analog and digital worlds that we occupy, and we generally feel calmer and more at ease in the analog. Personally, because so much of my work is digital, in the analog world, I truly feel I can step back. If most of your work is digital, and you get stressed just so much as *looking* at your busy calendar app, you may find the same. If you find the opposite, and enjoy the efficiency the digital world brings, consider creating a separate calendar that you use only for time blocking. This way, you can show and hide this calendar when you want to focus on other contexts in your work and life.

Categorize your blocks between "focus sprints" and more "casual work." In some time blocks, you may want to hunker down and focus intensely on something you really want to get done. In others, you may wish to more casually engage with your work, worrying less about accomplishment and focusing instead on making steady progress. Consider labeling some blocks as "focus sprints" for more concentrated work and others as "casual work" for when you'll have a more relaxed focus. I find that labeling more aversive tasks as "casual" eliminates some of the aversion and time pressure I feel before and while engaging with them.

Consider "theming" your days. Most of us juggle a variety of tasks and projects from many different areas of work. For example, you may have work that you can categorize as planning, creation, and coordination. Or maybe your tasks can be broken down into advertising, networking, and launch planning categories. Maybe your work is best divided into teaching, research, and service duties. Regardless of what your main work themes are, it can be mentally tiring to constantly switch between categories like these—and we can also get a lot accomplished when we focus on just one for most of the day. Play around with defining a "theme" for your day. Even if some days are simply maker's days and others are manager's days, you may be surprised by how much you get done by remaining in one context throughout the day. Themes are also higher up the Intention Stack— closer to your priorities than your daily intentions are—so they have a convenient way of guiding which goals, plans, and intentions you focus on throughout the day.

Time blocking and practicing sequential productivity can be remarkably helpful tactics for remaining intentional in each moment. However, it's also possible to become more intentional over longer time frames. Let's get to tactics for that now.

THE RULE OF THREE

As I hope you've come to see, intentionality, the driving force behind goal attainment, is a complex and beautiful topic. Yet, for as complex as it can be, becoming more intentional is rather simple. First, we must step back. Then, we must choose where to go.

Sequential productivity and time blocking are ways through which we can do this throughout our day. Farther up the Intention Stack, intentionality remains vital, and the more intentions we set—and the more often we reconnect with those intentions—the more progress we will make toward our goals. The key is to determine, alongside what we wish to accomplish, how our goals will flow into one another. The intentions we set across different time frames won't always be connected with one another, but the more they are, the more likely it is we'll achieve our goals. Explicitly taking time to reflect on the ways our intentions nest inside one another allows us to see more of the Intention Stack in our planning.

We have already done this with the goals we have set, but we can also do the same for our intentions that don't contribute to predefined goals. This kind of reflection exercise helps us connect not only with our individual intentions but also with *why* we set those intentions in the first place.

My favorite ritual for this is exceptionally straightforward. In sharing this rule, I'm going to again step a tad on the surface area of what I've covered in previous books; after all, my favorite intention-setting ritual is also my favorite prioritization ritual, and it may well be my absolute favorite productivity ritual. (I'll be quick in case you've heard me talk about it before.)

The ritual is called the rule of three. First, you pick a time frame—like each day, or the week or month ahead. Then, you put yourself in the shoes of your future self and ask: By the time this day is done, **what three things will I want to have accomplished**?

That's it.

The rule works just as well every week, month, quarter, and year. You name the timeline, and the rule will help you reflect across it. If you're a student who divides your time into semesters, it'll work across those timelines. If you're a salesperson who divides your year up into quarters, it'll work for you as well. The beauty of the rule is how it allows your intentions to flow into one another.

For example, I like to define my work and personal intentions at the start of each day, as well as each week alongside my goal review. This takes just a few minutes. But with the ritual, my intentions can funnel into one another. Because I set my weekly intentions during my goal review, I can decide on the main three goals I want to pull down into that week. I find that this helps me narrow my focus and make greater progress. Then, each day, I can look not only at what I *have* to get done (the stored intentions on my to-do list) but also at what I *want* to get done by considering how I can bring my weekly goals to fruition on a daily basis. If I'm time blocking that day, I can also make sure to schedule a chunk of time for those goals as well.

Three is somewhat of a magical number when it comes to prioritization. Because you can pick only three intentions—whether every day, week, month, quarter, or year—you really have no choice but to select which are the most important to you. In doing so, you practice task prioritization while working smarter. Research also shows we can easily hold three things in our mind at once.[4] This means that with the rule, you'll actually remember your broader intentions as you go about your day.

The true power of these rituals is in regularly taking a step back to define what your priorities—and goals—should be in the first place. Stepping back, you sharpen your axe, considering the best tree to chop down—instead of just hacking away at the one right in front of you.

As with sharpening an axe, setting intentions is a skill you will get better at over time. Do your best to choose the three most important and impactful things you want to get done. Lead with intention, and productivity will follow.

THREE WAYS TO GET STARTED

Throughout the previous chapters, we've talked about how it is possible to create goals that are aligned with what we truly value, ensuring that they're not only more motivating but also true to who we are.

In this chapter, we stepped aside from the Intention Stack, working our way from the bottom up, to connect our daily actions—and intentions—with our goals, so we can make greater progress toward them.

There is a beautiful synchronicity to be found in this alignment, when what you're currently doing is aligned not only with what you wish to accomplish but also with what you value.

After you set your intentions, you may dramatically over- and underestimate how long tasks will take. Maybe you'll schedule a one-hour block of time for writing a report that will end up taking three hours to complete. Or you'll block off an entire afternoon to deal with a thorny issue that it turns out you can resolve with one quick conversation. You may also over- or underestimate how much time, attention, and energy you'll have for dealing with your priorities in the first place. It will take time to settle into a rhythm and develop more of an awareness in your work.

Even after investing in one or two of these rituals for more than a decade, I have days when I'll misestimate how long something will take or the amount of resources I have to devote to that task. The solution is to once again hold your goals more loosely. You won't accomplish everything on your to-do list every day, and there's freedom in realizing that.

Here are a few ways I recommend getting started with the ideas in this chapter, to tie the ideas together in one tactical place.

1. **Start a daily intention-setting ritual**, whether in the morning or at the end of the workday, to define your daily intentions. Also consider choosing how you'll become more deliberate throughout your day, whether by time blocking, practicing sequential productivity, or even just a chime that goes off every hour on your phone or smartwatch that nudges you to take a second to consider what you're

working on. Working intentionally on a daily basis requires an island of intentional planning time like this. Over time, you can add (or subtract) from the ritual as you find tactics that provide you with the greatest payoff.

2. **Define the broader time frames across which you will set intentions—and carve out these islands of intention as well.** I personally set intentions every day, week, and month. In each of these sessions, I'll sit down with a tea or coffee to write down on paper what I'll want to accomplish in the time frame I'm planning for. I'll always keep my goal list open as I plan, so I can make sure to determine the next steps for the process goals I'm in the middle of attaining. By creating islands of intention across multiple time frames, you can plan out several layers of the Intention Stack on a regular basis. When setting intentions across more narrow time frames, like every week and day, pay special attention to how these intentions contribute to your broader goals. (They won't always, but you'll find that you have more latitude here than you think.)

3. **Remember that developing discipline takes time.** These techniques will help you to work and live more intentionally, but keep in mind that they will take a bit of time to settle into, as you develop an awareness of how long tasks in your work take and how much time, attention, and energy you have on a daily basis. Mind any negative self-talk that comes up as you get acquainted with your capacity for daily accomplishment. Then, when the next day, week, or month rolls around, be sure to reflect on how accurate your predictions were, so you can learn from and adjust how much you bite off every day. This self-reflective loop will pay dividends over time.

THE POWER OF INTENTION

Let me share a quick story from a few years back that illustrates the power and confidence that intentionality can bring. After publishing my first book, I got a very small taste of what it must be like to be a celebrity (at least from a time-management perspective, which is frankly the main angle I'm interested in). When the book launched, I was traveling around Toronto to chat with press about it and was being shuttled around the city by my wonderful Canadian book publicist at the time, Frances.

Looking back, the interviews are a blur, a successive stream of one conversation after another—some for video, some for audio, others for print. I can't remember anything I said that day. (I'd make a terrible celebrity.) But through it all, the thing I *do* remember is that I didn't have to worry about a single thing. When I needed to be somewhere across town to do another TV or radio hit, I didn't need to call an Uber: Frances had arranged for that. The moment I got hungry, food miraculously appeared. When my energy waned, tea materialized in front of me. It was pretty great. Instead of focusing on what I needed to do next, I could focus on being present in the interviews.

There is a certain indescribable kind of confidence that comes from knowing that whatever you're doing, that is what you need to be doing. So often as we work and live our lives, we're filled with doubt. *Am I working on the best possible thing? Is there somewhere else I should be? Is there something else I should be doing instead? What am I forgetting here?* This mental chatter can be costly, because it consumes precious attention we could be deploying into making progress—and being present enough to enjoy ourselves as we do. That day, because Frances took care of pretty much everything for me, I didn't have to worry about choosing what I'd get done next. She was my to-do list, my calendar, and above all else, she handled basically all the logistical overhead of my life.

In each moment, I could be truly present. And instead of being intentional about what I would do, I could instead be intentional about *how I would do it.* I freed up the attention that not thinking or caring about my to-do list brings.

The best word I can think of to describe how that made me feel is that I felt *free.*

To me, this experience illustrates the power and magic of intention. Most of us—myself included!—don't have someone like Frances around every day to tell us what to work on at any given moment. But as I've found, we can get surprisingly close. In a way, the techniques in this chapter—and the rest of the book—are tactics that we can utilize to become our own Frances. By predetermining what we spend time on from an island that is separate from the rest of our day, we give ourselves freedom and confidence in the moment that we can mobilize to make progress on what's important. The guilt, doubt, and worry we have surrounding how we spend our time evaporates. We settle into our tasks with confidence.

With every one of the goals on your list, there is a path through time and through your actions that will get you to the point of goal attainment. By identifying this path before you start pursuing your goal, you can be sure the path is clear for achieving it.

Along the way, you're sure to encounter plenty of obstacles—and opportunities. Perhaps at the start, your goal won't be clearly aligned with what you value. It may also be ugly and aversive, and lead you to procrastinate. Maybe you haven't invested enough time in identifying which process goal (or goals) will serve you best and accelerate your rate of progress.

Along your timelines of goal attainment, each of these obstacles will be worth dealing with in turn—and in the very next chapter I'll provide you with a checklist for how to do so. But you'll likely encounter many opportunities along the way as well. Most goals have a learning stage, where you feel out a goal to find the best approach to making progress. Over time, as you make repeated edits to your outcome and process goals, you'll find that you tiptoe closer and closer to making greater progress, with less effort. You'll find that your progress will become more meaningful as you reflect on your values and use this knowledge to edit your goals. This meaning will filter down to how you spend your time each day, too—especially as you practice some of the ideas in this chapter. You'll find shortcuts, extra pockets of motivation, and also recall tactics—in this book and beyond— that will make progress a lot more automatic.

All the while, you move closer and closer to attaining the goals on your list.

Goal attainment is a process that is unpredictable, messy, and sometimes full of hard work. But at its best, and at its core, it can also prove profoundly meaningful, while providing you more of what you want in both your workdays and your life.

I hope you consider the ideas and tactics I have shared in the book to be worthy of your time, attention, and energy.

And beyond any feeling of accomplishment—or any other value they may support—I hope they lead you to where you truly wish to go.

8

Putting It All Together

A SYSTEM FOR ACHIEVING
YOUR GOALS

We have covered a lot of ground over the course of this book. That's why, as we wrap things up, I've put together all the ideas and strategies we've learned into one final chapter. Consider this chapter a road map for setting and structuring your goals. If you wish, it can also serve as a handy guide for which pages to flip back to if you want to reconnect with certain ideas and tactics.

TACTICS FOR ATTAINING NEW GOALS

The process of following through on your goals can be broken down into four steps:

1. **Shape**: Define your goals to make them concrete.

2. **Act**: Set intentions to act on your goals across the Intention Stack.

3. **Edit**: Make *continual* improvements to how you define and view your goals over time.

4. **Maintain, Celebrate, and Reflect.**

Remember, goal attainment is not a linear process. You'll bounce among all the steps—especially as the timeline of goal attainment unfolds and you discover obstacles, challenges, and opportunities to accelerate your progress. Not to mention, when you are getting started with a goal, action should happen alongside editing. Actually acting on your goals provides you with critical feedback—including what you are doing wrong and right. This feedback naturally informs how you should edit your goals.

You won't want to practice every tactic here. There are a lot of them! Pick and choose the ones that feel right—and experiment with as many of them as you can to find the ones that provide you with the greatest return on your time.

Shape

First, **define your goal** (page 64). Don't be too set on getting this exactly right from the start—instead, see the starting shape of your goals as an iteration that you will develop, because many of your goals will evolve over time. To determine a goal's starting shape, **define its outcome and process goals** (page 66). Make sure to also define each goal's rate of progress, so you can mind this over time and make sure it's to your liking. Be sure to **nest your goals underneath or inside the values that they connect with**, as well (page 159). Hold your goals loosely, because you may need to revise some of them—if not most of them—over time. This lets you edit them so they're closer to what you want.

If a goal is aversive, make your process goals shorter in duration (page 74) and more specific (page 123). Also consider setting an if-then plan for *when*, *where*, and *how* you'll take action on your most aversive and challenging goals. **Mind the traps** that exist for setting goals, including setting goals that are sepia-toned (page 82) or that consume more resources than you have to offer (page 72). Make sure you will have enough time, attention, and energy for the goals you set.

Act

It's worth noting that you will act on and iterate on your goals at the same time. To make sure you take action toward your goals on a daily and weekly basis, **block off time for them** (page 192) or, if you want to get into the nitty gritty about managing your time and attention on a daily basis, **practice sequential productivity** (page 188). Consider also practicing **the rule of three** (page 197) to set intentions up and down your Intention Stack—while prioritizing what's on your plate. Whatever the number of intentions you set, just be sure to set them along the timelines you determine will allow you to act on your goals. You will also find that there are plenty of obstacles that will get in your way on the timeline of goal attainment. Anticipate obstacles ahead of time by **practicing mental contrasting** (page 86).

Edit

You will also need to edit and iterate on your goals, to make them more desirable and less aversive, more in line with what you value, and to zero in on what you are really after over time. There are countless ways to do this, and you obviously don't have to do them all. Pick and choose tactics to experiment with that feel like a good fit with your goals. For larger or more aversive goals, **chart out your desire**

curves (page 75) to identify any roadblocks that will get in your way on the road to goal attainment, based on your expected motivation over time and other external factors.

Depending on how aversive the goal is and will be, consider tackling that aversion in advance so you don't have to face it head-on. Mind the triggers of aversion a goal has.

- If a goal is boring, **make the goal more challenging** (page 103).

- If a goal is unpleasant, consider practicing **aversion journaling** (page 106) or making your goal **others-focused** (page 107), especially if the values you zeroed in on center around other people.

- If a goal is frustrating, **frame it as a learning goal** rather than as a performance goal (page 110).

- If a goal is far away in time, **track your progress** for attaining the goal over time in some way (page 113), consider setting **smaller nested goals** (page 116), **set rewards for milestones** that you will hit along the way (page 116), and **add some accountability** into the mix (page 116).

- If a goal is unstructured, consider **bribing yourself** with points for following through (page 122), **habit stacking** (page 121), or **adding some structure** to the goal in any way you can (page 117).

By making a goal less aversive, you make it more desirable. But there are specific tactics for increasing desire as well—even though desire is more emotional and a tad tougher to get tactical with. **Mind the social contagion you are experiencing around your goal** (page 134) by both bringing awareness to negative social contagion and doubling down on positive social contagion. Also tap into your self-reflective capacity to connect with how you feel about a goal. Try practicing **meditation** (page 149) or **journaling** (page 152) for this—

whether as a morning or evening habit or interstitially. Also consider **tracking your time** (page 173)—to see how much time you're spending across both your goals and values.

Finally, as you make changes to your goals, consider **setting up a trip wire or two** (page 177) in order to notice when you engage in habits that are counterproductive to your goal or so you can stop doing a negative goal in the first place. Trip wires are invaluable for goals intended for you to *stop* doing certain things.

Maintain, Celebrate, and Reflect

After you attain a goal, there is still a wee bit of following through left to be done. If you have been working toward a goal for a while, celebrate your achievement. Even if you don't want to, mark the occasion somehow. Consider locking in a goal by **turning it into a maintenance goal** (page 89). Be sure to also **reflect on how well things went**—you attained your goal, after all!—while also noting an improvement or two to make goal attainment easier for you the next time around. I recommend doing this through the **self-reflection rituals** we chatted about, like journaling (page 152), mind wandering around the idea (page 21).

Finally, **celebrate!** Add the goal to your **accomplishments list** (page xx), a great tactic to remind yourself of your efforts that also counterbalances feelings that you're not doing enough. Adding the badass thing you just did to some list is not enough, though. Look at your top values (page 46) and **come up with a fun and meaningful way to celebrate** the milestone that aligns with your values.

This is my second-to-last chapter that I'm writing in the book, and I hope to finish it and the book today. When I do, because I value pleasure/hedonism, I'm going to begin my celebrations by ordering a huge burrito.

TACTICS FOR DEVELOPING
A GOAL ATTAINMENT SYSTEM

In addition to strategies for attaining new goals, let's review the strategies we learned for developing a goal attainment system.

Begin by **creating an inventory of your current goals** (page 159) that you review regularly. Then, set up a **weekly goal review ritual** (page 88) so you can regularly check up on your goals, updating them where necessary. Be sure to also invest in the "Act" tactics mentioned above—like practicing time blocking or sequential productivity, along with an intention ritual like the rule of three.

The more connected with your values your goals are, the more meaningful and motivating they become. To ensure your goals are as deep and motivating as possible, **determine your top values** (page 46). And, depending on what your top values are, practice intentional indulgence (page 161), carve out a **values day** or just a values afternoon (page 169), while also **noticing any guilt** you experience when spending time on your top values (page 161).

Finally, in addition to the deliberate intentions you set, you have a bunch of default intentions, too. Mind these intentions, and learn to love them. You can notice and connect with your default intentions by practicing **mindfulness** (page 19), or take greater advantage of them by **wandering while on neural autopilot mode** (page 5).

Finally, **be mindful of how you relate to your default intentions in the first place** (page 18). Your default intentions are not only powerful—they also make you into the person you are. Connect with them before deciding on all the things you want to change and all the goals you want to achieve. Despite what you may want to change, you should do more to enjoy the default intentions that make you who you are.

Conclusion

Enjoying Your Defaults

Right before writing these words, I sat on the meditation cushion in my office for around thirty minutes, meditating and noticing the default thoughts flying around in my head. There were thoughts related to this book and how I should end it. There were thoughts about emails, upcoming travel, and how excited I am to grab Korean food with a friend tonight. There was also another random thought that my mind brought forward, some imaginary cringeworthy event that I physically tensed up to. (For the life of me I can't remember what it was. Thoughts are fleeting like that.)

When I first started meditating years ago, I recall being incredibly frustrated by the default nature of my mind. I would meditate off and on, going through cycles. For me, the frustration was influenced by how busy my mind was at a given time. When my mind was calm, I meditated more, but when my mind was busy, I would stop sitting entirely. There's an old Zen saying, of unknown origin, that directs us to sit in meditation for twenty minutes a day—unless we're too busy, in which case we should sit for an hour. I had heard this multiple times and liked it. Still, I did the opposite.

The turning point for me came when I made an effort to actually *enjoy* meditation and mindfulness. Instead of getting frustrated when my mind threw me off course, I used getting distracted as an excuse to get curious.

Where was my mind going to take me today?

What concerns are on my mind that I haven't yet connected with?

What thoughts will arise that will be surprising, funny, or even delightful?

If you've practiced meditation, you know that not every thought that comes up is fun. The practice can unearth some nasty stuff, conditioned thought patterns that can be difficult to turn away from as they come up. Other times, it's borderline comical how our mind refuses to focus on our breath. But as I have found, there is always room to be interested in the nature of our mind. The more curious I got, the more consistent I became in my practice.

Excited by this development, I started to bring this same curiosity to mindfulness, too, noticing the default actions I would take with inquisitiveness rather than with obligation. The practice became an opportunity to discover more about how I acted by default, to notice which small behaviors had become tiny habits for me over time. Mindfully walking, I'd notice how my feet just knew how to transfer my body weight from one to the other, repeatedly. I could also marvel at the default intentions that guided me through taking a shower, cooking breakfast, or going for a run. All without much or any thought.

Occasionally, a time would come when, tapping into my self-reflective capacity, I would want to do things differently from how these default intentions wanted me to. In some cases, this meant walking more slowly, to experience and enjoy each step. Other times, it meant choosing a healthier option for breakfast or taking a completely different route while running.

These proved to be exceptions, though.

More often than not, I learned to appreciate my defaults.

EARLIER IN THE BOOK, I shared how it is possible to take better advantage of your default intentions by becoming mindful of them. The final strategy I have for you, in this same spirit, is to *marvel* at them. This might sound like a weird tactic. But stick with me for a second.

It is a complex experience, being human. From the moment we are born, we enter a world in which we are conditioned to act in a certain way. Sometimes this conditioning comes from others—to not cry when we don't get our way, to eat what's in front of us, and to share what we have with our siblings. Other times, this conditioning forms because *we* took some action ourselves—after reflecting on life lessons we learned or because we became aware of some habit in ourselves that made us uncomfortable. So we decided to change. Our mind is the malleable product of both our conditions and choices.

After exploring the ideas and research I have shared in this book, I now truly believe that our default nature is worth marveling at rather than becoming frustrated by. There is a sense of wonder to be found in discovering all the ways we operate by default, including by noticing our default intentions and where they come from. Letting curiosity drive us to this wonderment, we can begin to admire the person we are—while appreciating on a deeper and more fundamental level who we are becoming as we follow through with our deliberate intentions.

Along the way to becoming more intentional, as you discover which defaults you want to break out of, your mind is sure to frustrate you. It will refuse to focus on and follow through with your goals. It will feel aversion to tasks you don't want to do. And you'll find plenty of things that you will want to change—especially if you have values that orient you toward improvement rather than conserving things to be the same as they already are.

But for every one thing about yourself you want to change, there are likely many, many more you do not. For starters, you in all likelihood love and believe in your most deeply held personal values. These are constructed out of your default intentions, which make you the person you are. You also likely have plenty of previous goals that have turned into habits for you, and that continue to produce dividends to this day. Maybe you take some of these for granted as well. And apart from the default intentions in your mind, you also likely have plenty to be grateful for in your life, work, and beyond. You're getting a lot right—far more than you need to change.

As I hope you have found throughout this book, intentionality is a fascinating subject that can also prove remarkably helpful in practice. By stepping back—and then choosing where to go from there—you can become more productive *and* experience more meaning in your days. Crucially, you can also tap into perhaps one of the most magnificent parts of being human: the fact that you can act with purpose, with deliberateness, with intention.

So step back and choose where to go. You won't just follow through and attain more of your goals. You'll also experience more meaning as you do.

My hope is that along the way you can appreciate not only who you are becoming but also, and far more important, the wonder of who you already are.

Acknowledgments

Even if you never intend to write a book, I highly recommend writing an acknowledgments section—whether for a specific project or for your life. Doing so is an exercise in gratitude: It's difficult to write one without becoming thankful for all the wonderful people who surround you.

I first want to thank my editors at Penguin Random House and Macmillan: Nina Rodríguez-Marty in the United States, Sarah St. Pierre in Canada, and Mike Harpley and Kate Walsh in the UK. One of my favorite things about writing a book is writing to the edge of my ability and then handing that work over to incredibly talented people who can push my words and ideas even further. This book is infinitely stronger because of your generous edits, Nina and Sarah. Thank you, Nina, Sarah, Mike, and Kate!

I also want to thank my literary agent, Lucinda Halpern. Lucinda has been my partner in publishing for more than ten years, through four books and one Audible Original. If it were not for Lucinda . . . well, let's just say I don't want to even entertain that line of thought. Lucinda is someone who really, truly cares—for all the right reasons. And one of the things I am most grateful for in my work is getting to work with her. Lucinda, thank you. I'm so grateful to have you in my corner! Thank you also to Michael Kaler for all of your help with coordination for this book!

ACKNOWLEDGMENTS

Creating a book takes a village, of course: editors, publishers, designers, marketers, and everyone in between. While my name gets to go on the cover, a book is a team sport. On that note, I'd also like to thank Chalista Andadari, Polly Beel, Magdalena Deniz, Charlotte Dixon, Kristina Fazzalaro, Molly Fessenden, Bridget Gilleran, Sue Kuruvilla, Josie Turner, Rachel Wainz, and Stuart Wilson. I refuse to pick favorites so I listed all of you in alphabetical order! Thank you, truly, for everything you have done to introduce readers to my work.

Thank you also to those in my strategy groups I meet with regularly. Including, again in alphabetical order: Anne Bogel, Katherine Chen, Nick Milo, Camille Pagán, Mike Schmitz, David Sparks, and Laura Vanderkam.

I also want to thank Luang Por Viradhammo. He is the monk from the first chapter who declined to be interviewed for the book. If there is one person from whom I have learned the most about the subject of human intentionality, it is him. Inside Luang Por Viradhammo is a well of wisdom. He is also responsible for suggesting the distinction between our default and deliberate intentions, which came out of his answer to my question. He can say in minutes what takes others years. With metta: Thank you.

Thank you also to Dana Hurley—my executive assistant extraordinaire who also helped out with some of the research for this book. I'm so thankful for your help, Dana, and for having you around to help out in general—I hope we get to work together for a super long time to come!

Thanks also to Anna, who designed the beautiful illustrations in this book. If you ever see something beautiful online that has my name attached to it, Anna likely designed it. I'm so grateful for your help, Anna. (And hi, Chris and Kai!)

I also want to thank my wife, Ardyn. Behind a lot of authors is a patient spouse—and this is also the case with me. When I write a book, I often get caught up in a web of my own thoughts and am not as present as would be ideal (despite all the meditation). That was especially true with this book. I'm so grateful for you, Ardyn. You're a badass, and I love you.

I also want to thank my high school economics teacher, Mr. Gord Moran. Wild and quirky, Gord was a treasure at the school I went to. The walls of his classroom were famously adorned with a great number of clocks (he appropriately called his room the Clockatorium). He used to call up the parents of any student who got higher than a certain grade on his tests to tell them how well the student did. In high school, I was a nerdy class clown. But more than almost anyone else, Gord saw through this to help me grow in the ways I most needed to. He, in large measure, also led me to my fascination with productivity. Gord, my books are in part your fault. We'll miss you.

Finally, thank you to you, for not only reading this book but also for making it to the end of the acknowledgments (of all places). I write books like this to benefit readers like you. Thank you for taking the time to read and support my work. Truly—it means more to me than you know. I hope you have found the ideas in this book helpful and interesting, and that they benefit you for some time to come.

Notes

A Quick AI Statement

1. Neal, David T., Wendy Wood, Jennifer S. Labrecque, and Phillippa Lally. "How Do Habits Guide Behavior? Perceived and Actual Triggers of Habits in Daily Life." *Journal of Experimental Social Psychology* 48, no. 2 (2012): 492–98, doi.org/10.1016/j.jesp.2011.10.011.

0. Elusive Goals

1. Glasspiegel, Ryan. "Wayne Gretzky Pays Homage to Michael Scott's Famous Stolen 'Office' Quote." *New York Post*, May 6, 2022. nypost.com /2022/05/06/wayne-gretzky-pays-homage-to-michael-scotts-stolen-quote.

1. The Intention Stack

1. Glück, Louise. *Proofs and Theories: Essays on Poetry.* Ecco Press, 1994.
2. Heslin, Peter A., and Karyn L. Wang. "Determinants of Goals." In *New Developments in Goal Setting and Task Performance,* edited by Edwin A. Locke and Gary P. Latham, 133–46. Psychology Press, 2013.
3. Heslin and Wang, "Determinants of Goals," 133–46.
4. Camerer, Colin F., and Xiaomin Li. "Neural Autopilot and Context-Sensitivity of Habits." *Current Opinion in Behavioral Sciences* 41 (2021): 185–90, doi.org/10.1016/j.cobeha.2021.07.002.
5. Duhigg, Charles. *The Power of Habit: Why We Do What We Do in Life and Business.* Random House, 2014.
6. Whether we truly have the "will" to craft original, deliberate intentions is a debate for a less pragmatic book. My quick take, if you're curious, is that

we cannot truly craft original intentions. But at the risk of getting overly philosophical (and Buddhist-y), in my view this doesn't matter as much as we think. We can *observe* our mind both forming intentions and generating thoughts in response to what happens around us. We can also observe it forming more complex, deliberate intentions in response to a more complex set of cues and conditions. But in my view, this capacity for observance ought to be enough. This is who we are at our core: We are the "observer" who is able to step back from the activity of our mind. One of the functions (features) of our mind is simply to craft intentions for us. So, while we may not have "free will," we do have this capacity of "free observance." We can always notice what our mind (our brain) is up to and which actions it is leading us to take.

7. Marino, Lori, Richard C. Connor, R. Ewan Fordyce, Louis M. Herman, Patrick R. Hof, Louis Lefebvre, David Lusseau, et al. "Cetaceans Have Complex Brains for Complex Cognition." *PLoS Biology* 5, no. 5 (2007), doi.org/10.1371/journal.pbio.0050139.

8. Baird, Benjamin, Jonathan Smallwood, and Jonathan W. Schooler. "Back to the Future: Autobiographical Planning and the Functionality of Mind Wandering." *Consciousness and Cognition* 20, no. 4 (2011): 1604–11.

9. de Bruin, E. I., J. E. van der Zwan, and S. M. Bogels. "A RCT Comparing Daily Mindfulness Meditations, Biofeedback Exercises, and Daily Physical Exercise on Attention Control, Executive Functioning, Mindful Awareness, Self-Compassion, and Worrying in Stressed Young Adults." *Mindfulness* 7, no. 5 (2016): 1182–92.

10. Baird, Smallwood, and Schooler, "Back to the Future,"1604–11.

2. Values

1. Nin, Anaïs. *Seduction of the Minotaur.* Swallow Press, 1961.

2. Sagiv, Lilach, Sonia Roccas, Jan Cieciuch, and Shalom H. Schwartz. "Personal Values in Human Life." *Nature Human Behaviour* 1 (2017): 630–39, doi.org/10.1038/s41562-017-0185-3.

3. Sagiv et al., "Personal Values in Human Life," 630–39.

4. Schwartz, Shalom H. "Universals in the Content and Structure of Values: Theoretical Advances and Empirical Tests in 20 Countries." *Advances in Experimental Social Psychology* 25 (1992): 1–65, doi.org/10.1016/S0065 -2601(08)60281-6.

5. Schwartz, Shalom H., Jan Cieciuch, Michele Vecchione, Eldad Davidov, Ronald Fischer, Constanze Beierlein, Alice Ramos, et al. "Refining the Theory of Basic Individual Values." *Journal of Personality and Social Psychology* 103, no. 4 (2012): 663–88, doi.org/10.1037/a0029393.

6. Schwartz, Shalom H. "An Overview of the Schwartz Theory of Basic Values." *Online Readings in Psychology and Culture* 2, no. 1 (2012): 11–20, doi .org/10.9707/2307-0919.1116.

7. Napier, Jaime L., Julie Huang, Andrew J. Vonasch, and John A. Bargh. "Superheroes for Change: Physical Safety Promotes Socially (But Not Economically) Progressive Attitudes Among Conservatives." *European Journal of Social Psychology* 48 (2018): 187–95, doi.org/10.1002/ejsp.2315.

8. Schwartz, "An Overview of the Schwartz Theory," 11–20.

9. Sagiv, Lilach, and Shalom H. Schwartz. "Value Priorities and Subjective Well-Being: Direct Relations and Congruity Effects." *European Journal of Social Psychology* 30, no. 2 (2000): 177–98, doi.org/10.1002/(SICI)1099 -0992(200003/04)30:23.0.CO;2-Z.

10. Sagiv et al., "Personal Values in Human Life," 630–39.

11. Sagiv et al., "Personal Values in Human Life," 630–39.

12. Sagiv et al., "Personal Values in Human Life," 630–39.

13. Hofstede, Geert. *Culture's Consequences: Comparing Values, Behaviors, Institutions, and Organizations Across Nations.* Sage Publications, 2001.

14. Sagiv et al., "Personal Values in Human Life," 630–39.

15. Sagiv et al., "Personal Values in Human Life," 630–39.

16. Sagiv et al., "Personal Values in Human Life," 630–39.

3. Goal Editing

1. Brahm, Ajahn. "Am I Good Enough?" YouTube, April 28, 2017, 1:06:05, youtube.com/watch?v=b2mWuCk70Ck.

2. Doran, George T. "There's a S.M.A.R.T. Way to Write Management's Goals and Objectives." *Management Review* 70, no. 11 (1981): 35–36. community .mis.temple.edu/mis0855002fall2015/files/2015/10/S.M.A.R.T-Way -Management-Review.pdf.

3. Swann, Christian, Patricia C. Jackman, Alex Lawrence, Rebecca M. Hawkins, Scott G. Goddard, Ollie Williamson, Matthew J. Schweickle, Stewart A. Vella, Simon Rosenbaum, and Panteleimon Ekkekakis. "The (Over)use of SMART Goals for Physical Activity Promotion: A Narrative

Review and Critique." *Health Psychology Review* 17, no. 2 (2023): 211–26, doi.org/10.1080/17437199.2021.2023608.

4. Swann et al., "The (Over)use of SMART Goals," 211–26.

5. Epton, Tracy, Sinead Currie, and Christopher J. Armitage. "Unique Effects of Setting Goals on Behavior Change: Systematic Review and Meta-Analysis." *Journal of Consulting and Clinical Psychology* 85, no. 12 (2017): 1182–98, doi.org/10.1037/ccp0000260.

6. "Quote Origin: To Cut Down a Tree in Five Minutes Spend Three Minutes Sharpening Your Axe." *Quote Investigator*, March 29, 2014. quoteinvestigator.com/2014/03/29/sharp-axe.

7. Allen, David. *Getting Things Done: The Art of Stress-Free Productivity*. Penguin Books, 2015.

8. Latham, Gary P., and Edwin A. Locke. "Self-Regulation Through Goal-Setting." *Organizational Behavior and Human Decision Processes* 50, no. 2 (1991): 212–47, doi.org/10.1016/0749-5978(91)90021-K.

9. Dillard, Annie. *The Writing Life*. Harper Perennial, 1989.

10. Bailey, Pippa, Susan Purcell, Javier Calvar, and Alex Baverstock. "Actions & Interventions for Weight Loss." Ipsos, January 18, 2021. ipsos.com/sites/default/files/ct/news/documents/2021-01/actions-and-interventions-for-weight-loss.pdf.

4. Ugly Goals: Lowering Aversion

1. Zhang, Shunmin, Tom Verguts, Chenyan Zhang, Pan Feng, Qi Chen, and Tingyong Feng. "Outcome Value and Task Aversiveness Impact Task Procrastination Through Separate Neural Pathways." *Cerebral Cortex* 31, no. 8 (2021): 3846–55, doi.org/10.1093/cercor/bhab053.

2. Healthwise Ottawa. "What Are YOU Waiting For? Procrastination Deconstructed." *Carleton Newsroom* (blog), September 20, 2012. newsroom.carleton.ca/archives/2012/09/20/what-are-you-waiting-for-procrastination-deconstructed.

3. Steel, Piers. "The Nature of Procrastination: A Meta-Analytic and Theoretical Review of Quintessential Self-Regulatory Failure," *Psychological Bulletin* 133, no. 1 (2007): 65– 94, doi.org/10.1037/0033-2909.13. 65–94.

4. Hesiod. *Works and Days*, translated by Gregory Nagy, Center for Hellenic Studies (Harvard University), accessed August 25, 2025, https://chs.harvard.edu/primary-source/hesiod-works-and-days-sb.

5. Van Eerde, Wendelien, and Katrin B. Klingsieck. "Overcoming Procrastination? A Meta-Analysis of Intervention Studies." *Educational Research Review* 25 (2018): 73–85, doi.org/10.1016/j.edurev.2018.09.002.

6. Steel, "The Nature of Procrastination," 65–94.

7. Blunt, Allan K., and Timothy A. Pychyl. "Task Aversiveness and Procrastination: A Multi-Dimensional Approach to Task Aversiveness Across Stages of Personal Projects." *Personality and Individual Differences* 28, no. 1 (2000): 153–67, doi.org/10.1016/S0191-8869(99)00091-4.

8. Van Eerde and Klingsieck. "Overcoming Procrastination?," 73–85, doi .org/10.1016/j.edurev.2018.09.002.

9. Steel, "The Nature of Procrastination," 65–94.

10. Epton, Tracy, Sinead Currie, and Christopher J. Armitage. "Unique Effects of Setting Goals on Behavior Change: Systematic Review and Meta-Analysis." *Journal of Consulting and Clinical Psychology* 85, no. 12 (2017): 1182–98, doi.org/10.1037/ccp0000260.

11. Steel, "The Nature of Procrastination," 65–94.

12. Epton et al., "Unique Effects of Setting Goals on Behavior Change," 1182–98.

13. Dweck, Carol S. "Motivational Processes Affecting Learning." *American Psychologist* 41, no. 10 (1986): 1040–48, doi.org/10.1037/0003-066X.41.10 .1040.

14. Elliot, Andrew J., and Holly A. McGregor. "A 2 X 2 Achievement Goal Framework." *Journal of Personality and Social Psychology* 80, no. 3 (2001): 501–19, doi.org/10.1037/0022-3514.80.3.501.

15. Zhang, Shunmin, and Tingyong Feng. "Modeling Procrastination: Asymmetric Decisions to Act Between the Present and the Future." *Journal of Experimental Psychology: General* 149, no. 2 (2020): 311–22, doi.org/10 .1037/xge0000643.

16. Zhang and Feng, "Modeling Procrastination," 311–22.

17. Gollwitzer, Peter M., and John A. Bargh. "Two Routes to the Self-Regulation of Motivation and Goals." In *Motivation Science: Controversies and Insights*, edited by Mimi Bong, Johnmarshall Reeve, and Sung-il Kim, 183–90. New York: Oxford University Press, 2023.

18. Gollwitzer and Bargh. "Two Routes to the Self-Regulation of Motivation and Goals," 818.

19. Webb, Thomas L., and Paschal Sheeran. "Does Changing Behavioral Intentions Engender Behavior Change? A Meta-Analysis of the Experimental

Evidence." *Psychological Bulletin* 132, no. 2 (2006): 249–68, doi.org/10.1037/0033-2909.132.2.249.

5. Attractive Goals: Increasing Desire

1. Nietzsche, Friedrich. *Beyond Good and Evil: Prelude to a Philosophy of the Future.* Translated by Helen Zimmern. 1886. Reprint, Project Gutenberg, 2009. gutenberg.org/files/4363/4363-h/4363-h.htm.
2. Perugini, Marco, and Richard P. Bagozzi. "The Role of Desires and Anticipated Emotions in Goal-Directed Behaviours: Broadening and Deepening the Theory of Planned Behaviour." *British Journal of Social Psychology* 40, no. 1 (2001): 79–98, doi.org/10.1348/014466601164704.
3. Ajzen, Icek. "The Theory of Planned Behavior." *Organizational Behavior and Human Decision Processes* 50, no. 2 (1991): 179–211, doi.org/10.1016/0749-5978(91)90020-T.
4. Sampson, Tony D. "Contagion Theory Beyond the Microbe." *CTheory*, January 11, 2011, journals.uvic.ca/index.php/ctheory/article/view/14968.
5. Christakis, Nicholas A., and James H. Fowler. "The Spread of Obesity in a Large Social Network over 32 Years." *New England Journal of Medicine* 357, no. 4 (2007): 370–79, doi.org/10.1056/NEJMsa066082.
6. Christakis, Nicholas A., and James H. Fowler. "Social Contagion Theory: Examining Dynamic Social Networks and Human Behavior." *Statistics in Medicine* 32, no. 4 (2013): 556–77, doi.org/10.1002/sim.5408.
7. Shalizi, Cosma Rohilla, and Andrew C. Thomas. "Homophily and Contagion Are Generically Confounded in Observational Social Network Studies." *Sociological Methods & Research* 40, no. 2 (2011): 211–39, doi.org/10.1177/0049124111404820.
8. Perugini and Bagozzi. "The Role of Desires and Anticipated Emotions."
9. Bolte, Annette, and Thomas Goschke. "Intuition in the Context of Object Perception: Intuitive Gestalt Judgments Rest on the Unconscious Activation of Semantic Representations." *Cognition* 108, no. 3 (2008): 608–16, doi.org/10.1016/j.cognition.2008.05.001.

6. Deeper Goals

1. Thoreau, Henry David. *Walden, or, Life in the Woods.* Ticknor and Fields, 1854.

2. Mark, Gloria, Shamsi T. Iqbal, Mary Czerwinski, Paul Johns, and Akane Sano. "Neurotics Can't Focus: An *In Situ* Study of Online Multitasking in the Workplace." Paper presented at the 2016 CHI Conference on Human Factors in Computing Systems: San Jose, California, May 2016. dl.acm .org/doi/10.1145/2858036.2858202.

3. Parsons, Talcott. *The Social System*. Routledge & Kegan Paul, 1951.

4. Housel, Morgan (@morganhousel). "A Lot of Financial Debates Are Just People with Different Time Horizons Talking over Each Other." X, April 17, 2022, 8:32 p.m. x.com/morganhousel/status/1515850809866526722 ?lang=en.

7. Intention Rituals

1. Seneca. *Ad Lucilium Epistulae Morales*. Translated by Richard M. Gummere. Letter LXXI. Loeb Classical Library, 1920. Accessed via the Internet Archive. archive.org/details/in.ernet.dli.2015.185484.

2. Lavie, Peretz, Jacob Zomer, and Daniel Gopher. "Ultradian Rhythms in Prolonged Human Performance." United States Army Research Institute for the Behavioral and Social Sciences, 1995, researchgate.net/publication /235129211_Ultradian_Rhythms_in_Prolonged_Human_Performance.

3. Strelca, Aiva. "Productivity Research, Experiments, and Statistics: Desk-Time's Best Findings." *DeskTime* (blog), December 13, 2021. desktime.com /blog/productivity-research.

4. McVay, Jennifer C., and Michael J. Kane. "Conducting the Train of Thought: Working Memory Capacity, Goal Neglect, and Mind Wandering in an Executive-Control Task." *Journal of Experimental Psychology: Learning, Memory, and Cognition* 35, no. 1 (2009): 196-204, doi.org/10 .1037/a0014104.

Index

NOTE: *Italic page locators* indicate illustrations.

Discover more from author

CHRIS BAILEY

SCAN ME
or visit
sites.prh.com/chrisbailey-links

PRH collects and processes your personal information on scan. See prh.com/notice.

🐧 PENGUIN BOOKS

eady to find your next great read? Let us help. Visit prh.com/nextread